MW00944630

RESCUED FROM THE
Pit

Healing from Schizophrenia

An Autobiographical Novel

ROSEMARY ROSS

Rescued from the Pit
Healing from Schizophrenia
by Rosemary Ross

Printed in the United States of America

ISBN 9781498403795

Edited by Xulon Press.

www.xulonpress.com

This book is dedicated to my late beloved son, Kenneth, my late wonderful mother, Helen, and my very good friend, Mathieu, who is like a grandson to me and who typed and help me write this book.

Most persons' names and the locations of events
in this book have been changed to help protect
identities.

TABLE OF CONTENTS

Chapter One

NO ESCAPE

Miami, 1963

I was finally alone in my mother's and my tiny Coconut Grove apartment. I stood in our small dining alcove at the black, wrought iron and glass dining table. I counted brown sleeping capsules as I swallowed them. "One, two, three, four … fifty-six, fifty-seven, fifty-eight … seventy-five, seventy-six, seventy-seven." There, that should be enough, I decided, as I felt the last capsule go down my throat.

The empty glass in my hand felt so heavy I couldn't hold it. It fell to the floor, shattering and leaving glass fragments all over the tile. The walls seemed to weave around me even though I thought I was standing still. The floor and ceiling kept changing places.

I've got to go to the park, I thought, but my legs felt like jello, they were wobbling so! I started walking the best I could, unable to feel the glass fragments scraping against my bare feet. Somehow I made it the three blocks to the park. As I stumbled there, all I could feel was a great heaviness weighing me down. I couldn't see anything, not people, buildings, or landscapes; my world was black.

Sometime later, as I lay in a hospital bed recovering from my suicide attempt, I still saw black. But, I felt the presence of an absolute power, the essence of love and peace. I was experiencing so much peace. The only way I could explain this feeling was that I believed I was with God. I felt His presence surrounding me. It enveloped me as though He were holding me in His arms. I no longer felt the pain that caused me to take seventy-seven sleeping capsules. I only knew I wanted to stay right there, with Him.

"Dear God, can I stay here with you?"

Even as I asked that question, I could feel something pulling me back to earth. I found myself opening my eyes slightly and seeing someone dressed in blue. But my head felt heavy, and I was so tired. I found myself back with the power I believed to be God.

I tried again to speak to Him. "God, please let me stay here with You. I don't want to go back to earth and feel the way I felt there."

Still, the awakening continued. I opened my eyes for a second time, and saw the same blue uniform on a blonde-haired girl, walking past me. Then the heaviness returned and, once again, I was back with God. "Dear God," I said, "do I have to go back to earth? Is it because of my baby—because he needs me?"

God never answered me directly, and soon I awoke completely.

"Liz! Thank God! You're back with us!" I saw my mother Emily standing there smiling at me. "I've been praying so hard for you! Three doctors have been working frantically to save your life. You've been in a coma for the past two days. Seeing you alive is so wonderful! I'm so relieved."

I looked around me and saw I was in a hospital bed. The stark white walls needed paint, and I saw an open door leading to a bathroom. I saw a young woman with blonde hair, dressed in a blue uniform. I decided she must be a nurse of some sort; she must have been the person I'd seen as I was coming to.

I saw another patient in a different bed. She appeared to be an older woman with gray hair, wearing a hospital gown with a faint flower design. I looked down at my body, wondering what I was wearing, and saw I had on a similar gown. I looked back at Mother.

"I guess I'm also glad to be alive, Mom. Maybe I do want to live. But just a few minutes ago I felt like I was with God. With Him, it seemed like I had escaped. Now that I'm awake, I'm so scared, discouraged, and miserable. It's like I'm 'miserating,' the only word I can come up with to describe the way I feel. I don't just exist; I miserate. My mental illness is back. I feel depressed all the time, trying to cope with everything and get well. Will my nightmare world of schizophrenia ever end? Why do I have schizophrenia?"

Chapter Two

HAPPY BEGINNINGS

Chicago, 1945

I ran up the front sidewalk, all the way from the street to the front door of our very large and very old house. I saw Grandoo standing on the porch, holding out his arms and watching me.

"Here I am, Elizabeth!"

I ran to Grandoo and jumped, trying to land in his arms. Immediately, I felt his soft suit pressing on my body. Then he helped me down to the porch. At five years of age, I didn't realize how weak he was at eighty.

"I'm sorry, Elizabeth," Grandoo said as we walked into the house. "I guess I'm getting older."

It was spring and there was no fire in Grandoo's living room fireplace. Grandoo went over to his favorite chair, sat down, and picked up a large old book from his side table.

"Come and sit on my lap, Elizabeth," Grandoo said with a smile. "At least I think I can handle that!"

I ran over to Grandoo and climbed on his lap. He looked at me, still smiling. Cuddling up on Grandoo's lap was one of my favorite things to do, like eating butter by itself off a spoon in the kitchen.

My mother walked over to us, holding the big straw broom she was using to sweep the floor. Her face looked tired, and she didn't smile.

"Emily, don't you think young Elizabeth looks somewhat like the man in this picture?" Grandoo pointed to a picture of a man with long hair on the book's cover.

Mom looked at the picture, and smiled. "Well, I guess she does. Who is that man?"

"John Quincy Adams, an ancestor of Elizabeth's and mine."

"What's an-cess-ter?" I asked Grandoo.

"It is a person who is related to you, like a great grandfather, who lived a long time ago and is no longer alive."

"You mean my an-cess-ter's on a book cover? That's neat!"

I looked out the window and saw the sunshine pushing back the clouds and shining in the house making it light up. I looked at Grandoo again. "You know what I want to do, Grandoo?"

"What's your heart's desire, Elizabeth?"

"I want to go to the drug store and buy some candy."

"Sure, Sweetheart. Go get your sweater, and we'll go."

I jumped off Grandoo's lap and ran toward the stairs to climb them and get my sweater from my bedroom. The old floors of Grandoo's house squeaked beneath my feet as I started up the steps. Before I reached the top of the stairs, I heard knocking on our front door. I walked back down the steps to the front door and saw Grandoo standing there with a woman.

The woman was tall, with soft-looking skin, but she had lines and wrinkles on her face. The color of her skin was white, kind of like the white milk the milkman brought us in his truck every day. Her eyes seemed blue, like the sky when there are no clouds.

Her hair was white like Grandoo's, so I decided she must be old, too.

"Come on in, Cousin Jennifer," I heard Grandoo say. "How are you?"

"Oh, I'm fine, Jonathan, just fine. You're the one I'm worried about."

"Why is that?"

She looked at me and back at Grandoo. "Well, I see that child is still here. And I presume her mother continues to live here, as well?"

"Why yes, Jennifer, my granddaughter Elizabeth and her mother Emily are still here with me, enriching my life. I was just commenting about the way Elizabeth resembles our ancestor, John Quincy Adams."

"Oh, but Jonathan, what about your reputation, and our Scott family's reputation?"

I didn't like the way this woman named "Jennifer" was talking to Grandoo. Why didn't she want me and Mom to live with him? I'd never before felt angry with any of Grandoo's friends or family, but this woman's words were upsetting me.

"But, Jonathan, I think you should find other living arrangements for Elizabeth and Emily. They've lived here too long, making it hard on you."

By this time, Cousin Jennifer was sitting on the old, gold, fancy couch, but Grandoo remained standing, looking at her angrily. I had never seen him look that way before.

"Jennifer, my decision in this matter involves changes you need to make, instead. You need to decide to accept Elizabeth and Emily and their place in our family and my home. For this is my home, and until you make those changes, you are not to visit me here. I will come visit you."

Cousin Jennifer stood with a jerk. The wrinkles on her face looked worse as she said, "Well, you certainly are touchy about this matter! I never expected you to talk this way to me. And, I'm not welcome here anymore? Yes! I will be leaving!"

Cousin Jennifer marched to the door and left.

I wasn't used to hearing anyone argue, especially not with Grandoo. He never even spoke like he was mad or upset.

I don't want to feel bad about Cousin Jennifer anymore, I thought. I want to be happy again with my grandoo.

"Grandoo, are we still going to the drugstore for candy?"

Grandoo turned around and saw me standing behind him. He smiled, as he said, "Yes, Sweetheart, go get your sweater. It's warm outside, but there's a chill in the breeze."

"Oh, I forgot my sweater. Okay!"

As I climbed the stairs to the second floor, I thought how happy I was that Cousin Jennifer was no longer in our home. Life was so much fun with Grandoo; I didn't want anything to change. He's my grandoo, and he won't let anyone bother me or Mom, I decided.

We walked together to the drug store, as we had so many times before, and I bought some of my favorite candies!

That night in bed before I fell asleep I received my usual nightly visit. "The Jack of Diamonds, the Queen of Hearts, and the King of Spades. All of you imaginary card friends came to visit me again tonight! How are you? You look so colorful and pretty. Did you have a good day?" The royal visitors didn't answer me. "I guess I'd better say goodnight to you now and go to sleep." My card visitors left, as quickly as they'd appeared. They'd silently danced before my eyes, in all of their colorful clothes. I no longer saw them as I fell asleep.

So went life in my grandoo's 100-year-old mansion, our home, with two main floors, seven fireplaces, nine bedrooms, an attic, basement, and huge living room with shelves of books covering two long walls. This was the only life I'd ever known, and I was very happy. I hoped nothing would ever happen to change our lives.

***

When I had just turned seven, I was a student in the first grade at an elementary school in Chicago. I liked school a lot. Learning to read was exciting, and I had fun with the other kids in school. Mom and I continued living with my grandoo, retired Dr. Jonathan Scott.

I came home from school one Friday afternoon in December. It was cold, and I felt the warmth from the living room fireplace and our furnace throughout my body. I shook the snowflakes off my galoshes as I took them off. Then off came my coat, cap, and scarf.

My skin prickled with excitement as I thought about Christmas coming. I wondered where Mom was, because I wanted to ask her about getting a big Christmas tree this year. I walked into our dining room and saw her setting the table for dinner.

"Hi, Mom!"

"Hi, Honey!"

Mom put the soup tureen she was holding on the table, right in the center. I knew she did that so all of us could reach some of her delicious chicken noodle soup. Looking at the dishes on the table, I could see they were the same white-and-blue flowered antique china our Scott family had used ever since my father Kenneth and his brothers were young boys. This scene increased my warm feelings, and I was glad to be a Scott.

Mom started placing our family's sterling silverware on the table. I decided this was my chance to ask her about a Christmas tree.

"Mom, can we have a big, big Christmas tree this year?"

"Oh, I hope so, Elizabeth! After Christmas we'll be moving to Washington State, a long ways away, so

I do want this Christmas to be one we'll remember. It's almost Christmas! I'll ask your grandoo."

I couldn't figure out what Mom meant about moving. "What do you mean, Mom?"

"I've been wanting to talk with you about this. Do you remember me telling you about my sister Ann and her family?"

"I guess so."

"Ann wants us to move out west and live near her."

"But Grandoo and all our family live here in Chicago!"

"Your father Ken's family, Elizabeth, not my family. My sister and brothers don't live in Illinois."

"Where do they live?"

"You'll remember; my brothers live not too far from here. Gerald lives in Iowa, and Joseph in Nebraska. You wouldn't remember them because the last time we've seen either of them or their families was when you were a baby. But Ann lives in Seattle, Washington, which is way out west, north of California."

"But, Mom, why do we have to leave Grandoo? Aren't you happy here?"

"Let's go sit in the living room, Elizabeth. I've finished setting the table."

We walked to the next room and sat on the antique couch in the front of the fireplace. At first, we were quiet, watching the flames dancing along the logs.

Mom did seem to look happier, I noticed, when talking about moving. I remembered when she told me how my father didn't want to have a child. He didn't want me to be born, but she wanted me. I'd never met my father all these years. I had decided, however, that my father was the only person I ever hated. I hated him for not wanting me. I always wondered why. Wasn't I pretty enough? Was I dumb? I thought about this and it hurt, but I mainly thought about being happy with my beloved grandoo and the rest of our Scott family.

Then Mom spoke. I noticed her smile as she continued. "Ann is a nurse, Elizabeth, a public health nurse. She is just two years younger than me. We were always close growing up, and I miss her.

"I know you are happy here, but living with Ken's relatives is hard for me at times. Your grandoo is wonderful to both of us. I love him very much for that. But sometimes I feel less accepted by a few of our other Scott relatives here."

I didn't understand what Mom was talking about, but I could tell she would be happier with her own family. Still, I didn't like the idea of moving away from Grandoo. I loved him so much. Why couldn't we stay with him? But, Mom wanted to be close to her family. And, I loved Mom. I didn't want to lose her. I said, "Well, okay, Mom. I guess maybe we can move out west if it's that important to you. But, I'll really miss Grandoo and everyone here."

My cousins, aunts, and uncles all came over for a large Christmas dinner, and we had a huge tree! Then, after New Year's, Mom and I moved to Seattle.

Chapter Three

TO TALK BACK IS
TO DIE

Seattle, 1948

"Ha, Ha, Ha! That joke is funny, Carl. I'm glad you let me come with you and Mom when you go out. I get to hear all your funny jokes!"

Carl turned around from the front seat of the taxi to where Mom and I were sitting, and smiled at me.

"I'm glad you think my jokes are funny, Elizabeth. Maybe I can teach you how to tell jokes like me."

"Great, Carl! I want you to!"

"You're so much nicer to me than the people we met coming out here. One lady we stayed with would slap my hand with a ruler. Another woman we lived with made me stay down in her basement by myself. I didn't like those mean people!"

I brushed one of my ringlets out of my eye. My blond hair was turning light brown and getting longer. Mom had told me that the air in Washington State was wetter than the air in Chicago. She said that was the reason my curly hair was getting curlier.

Carl was still watching me, and I wondered why he looked at me so long. "You're such a pretty girl, Elizabeth. I would think everyone would want to be nice to you!" I looked at Carl. He was kind of handsome. I told Mom I wanted her to get married again so I could have a new daddy. I hoped she would marry Carl.

Mom had just started working at a radio station in Kenniltown, a small town located directly across Lake Washington from Seattle. She had a radio program she called, "Listen Ladies." She also wrote all the advertisements and managed the station office. Mom had studied radio broadcasting at Northwestern University while we lived with Grandoo.

During this time, Mom and I were living with a nice family in Kenniltown. Their daughter was my age, and we were becoming close friends.

Mom wanted to buy a small house in Kenniltown. I rode around with her and a realtor many days after school, looking at houses. One day, while riding around, I felt kind of strange. It seemed like my new world wasn't "real," but I wasn't in a fantasy world. I felt somewhere in between. This new world of mine in Kenniltown, was it real, or was my only real world back with Grandoo in Chicago? I wondered, can I cope with my new life? Before long, the eerie feelings left, and I was back in the car with Mom in my new city.

A few months later, Mom and Carl were married at the Congregational Church in Kenniltown. Mom looked so pretty as she took her vows, wearing her new green dress and standing next to Carl, my soon-to-be new daddy. Soon after the ceremony, Carl said to me, "Now that your mother and I are married, Elizabeth, you can call me 'Daddy.'"

"Yes," Mom said. "Carl is now your stepfather. Also, do you want to stay Elizabeth Scott, or do you want your last name to become Jones, since Jones is Carl's last name and my new last name? It's up to you."

"I'll go by 'Elizabeth Jones,' Mom, since that's your name now." I thought to myself, I have a new daddy and a new last name.

Mom bought a small, frame house in Kenniltown. She called it a "bungalow." She paid the down payment with some of the money Grandoo had given her. Our new home had two bedrooms, a kitchen, a living room, one bathroom, and a dining room. It sat on top of a steep hill and had both a lily pond and a beautiful rose garden in the side yard. There were French doors between the living room and dining room. On one wall of the living room stood a fireplace surrounded on both sides by built-in bookshelves. Soon the three of us moved in.

One evening, before I went to bed, Mom said, "Elizabeth, kiss your daddy good night." It probably won't be so bad, I thought, because when I'd kissed Grandoo good night, I'd always enjoyed him kissing me on my cheek and giving me a big hug.

I stretched up to kiss Daddy on his cheek, but he turned his head so we kissed with our lips. Then, something awful happened. Daddy put his tongue in my mouth! Yuck, I thought, why is he doing this? What kind of goodnight kiss is that? I didn't like that experience at all, but Daddy looked down at me and smiled.

For the next couple of evenings, I kissed Daddy good night, and he continued to kiss me the same way. As he did this, he appeared happy with me. Finally, one evening when Mom asked me to kiss Daddy, I couldn't stand it! I didn't know if she knew what was happening during those awful kisses, but I vowed I'd never kiss Daddy that way again!

"I won't, Mom. I won't! I won't kiss Daddy goodnight anymore!" I backed away from Daddy and moved closer to Mother. His pleased expression changed to a frown, and he glared down at me. He looked at me as if I'd betrayed him, and he hated me for it. Mom looked at me in surprise, but said, "All right, Sweetheart. If it bothers you, you don't have to kiss him."

A few nights later, I lay in bed trying to fall asleep. I heard talking in the dining room. Then the voices became louder and I realized it was Mom and Daddy arguing. I got out of bed and walked quickly to the dining room. When I reached Daddy I said, "Leave my mother alone! She's had enough problems already. You're not going to give her anymore!"

Daddy came at me with a wild look in his eyes. Before I could get away, he grabbed me by my neck and pinned me against the wall. His hands were cold and rough. I could feel myself beginning to pass out. "Stop it! Stop it, Carl! Stop doing that to Elizabeth, you're going to kill her," I heard Mom scream. She kept shouting those words until Daddy's glassy stare softened slightly.

He looked at Mom and said, "I'm not going to kill Elizabeth, Emily. I'm just teaching her a lesson!" As he slowly took his hands from my throat, I fell to the floor. My neck was throbbing as I gasped for air. Gradually my strength returned, and I stood up and walked near Mom, as far away from Daddy as I could get.

How can this be the same man who joked with me and treated me so well? I wondered. Now he's vicious and terrifying. I sure hope he never attacks me again. I'm only seven years old, so how would I be able get free from him?

The next day I went to school, as usual. But I kept thinking about the previous night's terror. It was a relief to be at school. At least Daddy couldn't get to me there.

The elementary school in Kenniltown was a pleasant place for me. Most of the teachers were easy to get along with, and I was doing well with my studies. It was a good haven for me, especially that day.

Mrs. Owens, our teacher, was reading to us. The room was quiet as we listened or at least pretended to listen. I wondered if any of the other students' parents were like Daddy, or if I was the only one who had to go home to such a terrible person. I envied my classmates and wished my grandoo awaited me at home instead of Daddy. I remembered Grandoo's great love for me and the wonderful life I'd had with him and Mom. Later, while walking the eight blocks home from school, I tried not to worry about facing Daddy at home.

When I reached our house, I noticed Daddy standing in the side yard working with the roses. I walked in the house and straight to my room, because I didn't want be around Carl until Mom arrived home.

When I heard Mom come home, I met her in our kitchen. "Hi, Mom! Did you have a good day at the station?" Mom looked so pretty. She wore an attractive suit she'd recently tailored for herself after taking a tailoring course at the Kenniltown Civic Center.

Before Mom could answer, Daddy yelled, "Get out of here, you son of a bitch! I want to talk to your mother, and we don't want you here!"

"Elizabeth can be here with us, Carl! How can you talk to her that way? That's no way to talk to a child!" Mom looked shocked at Carl's sudden outburst. Some of her prettiness faded, and her face showed worry.

"I thought we were going to eat dinner, Daddy," I said.

"Yes, we'll be ready to eat soon," Mom said. "Sit down at the table." Daddy and I sat down across from each other. I was frightened.

"Just who did you think you were last night, Elizabeth? What your mother and I were talking about didn't concern you at all. It was none of your goddamn business!"

"Carl, Elizabeth is my daughter and part of our family; whatever concerns me also concerns her."

"The hell it does! She's no damn good, anyway. She never will be any good. She's just like her father. Both of them are just no goddamn good!"

I couldn't believe what I was hearing. My whole world was crumbling. I'd rather not have any daddy than one as cruel as him, I thought. As I sat quietly eating dinner, I wondered, could Carl be right? Am I no good? I don't think he's right; that's not what Grandoo said about me. And, all my other relatives in Chicago thought I was a good girl. But now I can't go back and ask them. Daddy's the adult here, so maybe he's right. Oh, I hope not.

Chapter Four

MALES AND BETRAYALS

Kenniltown, 1951

Three years later, our family's life continued in Kenniltown, Washington, both good and evil. I'd been taking dancing lessons since I was eight. Dancing became a good outlet for me, and good exercise. It helped me work off some of the tensions I was feeling from my problems with Carl. Along with my dancing activities, I was also a Blue Bird and looking forward to becoming a Camp Fire Girl. One day while at a Blue Bird meeting, one of my girlfriends called me "Liz." I had never been called anything but Elizabeth before, but the name "Liz" seemed good because it was shorter.

I told Mom one day I liked the name "Liz," because it was not as long as "Elizabeth," and easier to say.

She replied, "Actually, 'Liz' is one of the nick-names for Elizabeth. It's usually the short version, but some girls also go by 'Beth.'"

"I like Liz the best. I want to be called that."

"Okay, Liz!"

My mother started calling me "Liz" all the time, but Carl never would. I decided that I would never honor Carl by calling him "Dad" or "Father." I always continued to call him "Daddy," because, when I started calling him that at his suggestion, I liked and respected him. But now I no longer had respect for him nor did I wish to call him by any other names.

Around that same time, Mom lost her job at the radio station in Kenniltown. The ownership changed, and all the staff was laid off. Mom decided not to apply for a job at a TV station in Seattle; most of her coworkers did apply and got jobs there. Mom had studied the new field of television at Northwestern University in Chicago, but now she worried about leaving me alone too much with Carl if she commuted between Seattle and Kenniltown. Instead she took a local job working for two doctors in Kenniltown.

When Mom was a young adult, she attended nursing school with her sister. She became ill after the first year, and her physician father took her out of the program. Her sister Ann completed her RN degree, and later became a public health nurse. Mom attended a conservatory of music for one year, and then studied secretarial science. Because of Mom's medical training and secretarial skills, she was able to work for a dermatologist during the Great Depression. Even in those times, she never had a problem finding work.

Even though Mother was not able to continue working in broadcasting, she very much enjoyed working for the two doctors in Kenniltown, who were father and son. They became good influences in our lives, which helped us as our problems continued with Carl.

One afternoon, after a troop meeting, I arrived home and saw Carl in the kitchen. "Where did you put my notebook, Elizabeth, when you 'cleaned up' our bedroom last weekend?" he demanded.

"I put all the stuff that was on your dresser in the top drawer."

"Oh, no you didn't! I looked there. All you ever do is lose my things when you 'clean up.' You're so damn stupid, Elizabeth. You'll never be able to get married. No man would want to marry a girl as stupid as you."

I felt as small as an insect. Carl certainly didn't think I was much good, even though I'd tried helping him.

"Don't ever clean up our bedroom again, Elizabeth. I don't need anyone as dumb as you helping me. Why don't you just go jump off a cliff somewhere? We'd all be better off if you did."

My feelings were jamming up inside of me. I couldn't cope with all of them. I won't think about all of this, I thought. I can't. He's too cruel. I'll try not to worry about Carl and everything he's saying to me.

All through the fifties there were incidents between Carl and me, which brought havoc to an otherwise enjoyable period of my youth. At least I could depend on one fact; Carl certainly spoke to me with fierce hatred.

An incident Mom told me about happened several times during their first years of marriage. Carl would say, "Emily, that son of a bitch, no-good daughter of yours is a streetwalker. I've seen her with men. I know about her."

"Wait a minute, Carl," she interrupted. "If you're calling Liz a son of a bitch, then that means you're calling me a bitch, and I don't like that. I don't believe Liz walks the streets, anyway. She's not like that."

"I'm not telling you you're a bitch, Emily. I'm just telling you that Elizabeth is no damn good and never will be. She's trying to break us up and end our marriage. I won't let her, though, the little shit-ass."

"Carl!" Mom said with a shocked look on her face.

"You'll see, Emily, Elizabeth will turn against you when she grows older, and then it'll be too late."

The idea of my trying to break up Mom and Carl's marriage was far from the truth. Several times during their marriage, Mom asked me if I thought she should divorce Carl. I always replied, "No, Mom, don't divorce Carl. He drinks too much now. I worry about him becoming an alcoholic if you leave him."

Mom told me she asked the senior doctor she worked for if she should divorce Carl, considering the way he treated me. He said it surely was a problem, but at least we had an intact family this way, so maybe it would be better to stay together. Therefore, considering what the doctor said and what I said, Mom didn't divorce Carl.

There continued to be incidents when I tried to help with the work around our home. I hoped Mom would let me learn some housekeeping; for instance, helping with washing the dishes. But Carl was there, and once again destroyed my chances.

"You get out of here, Elizabeth. You don't belong in here. Go to your room and leave us alone. We don't want you here. You're too stupid to do the dishes; you'd probably end up breaking them. Just get out of here, you little cock sucker."

I decided I'd like to learn how to mow the lawn with our manual lawn mower. Carl objected, saying, "You can't mow the lawn, Elizabeth. Do you think I'm stupid or something? You'd just wreck the lawn mower. Then we'd have to buy a new one." I did not offer again, but he often complained to Mom that I would never be able to be a good housewife because I didn't know how to take care of a house.

One Christmas I received several great presents. Mom's and Carl's name were on the tags; they read, "From Mom and Daddy." But I knew he had nothing to do with selecting or buying my gifts. Carl didn't enjoy Christmas. He was always complaining and wishing the day would end and Christmas would be over.

One Christmas day, I received some new games. With my hopes high, I approached Carl and asked him to help me learn how to play one. He responded, "Get away and leave me alone, you little son of a bitch. Can't you see I don't want to play your silly game? Now you've ruined my Christmas. Get away!" I couldn't understand how asking a simple favor of Carl could ruin his day, but I left him alone after that.

During another Christmas season, Carl and Mom were in the back yard, trying to get our Christmas tree into its stand. As I walked over to where they stood, I realized they were arguing about the way they should place the tree in the stand. Carl had an axe in his hand. He'd been chopping off the trunk of the tree to make it fit.

"Why don't you chop more off the trunk, Carl?" I heard Mom ask. "Then I think it will fit in the stand."

"No, Emily, this tree is no good. It won't work. We should have bought that other tree, the one I wanted."

Just then, I walked over to Mom and Carl. It was dark that evening. I could barely make out their forms by the back porch light. "Mom's right, Carl," I said. "I think you should chop more off the tree's trunk." As I said this to Carl, I turned around toward Mom with my back to him. I didn't notice his hand as he raised his axe and started to bring it down onto my head.

Suddenly I was startled to hear Mom scream, "No, Carl! Stop!" I turned around and saw Mom's hand on Carl's arm. She'd stopped him. She had saved my life. Carl, in a fit of rage, had attempted to kill me! The following morning he firmly denied the incident.

Mom told me, soon after Carl's fit of rage, that he had been married before they met. She'd heard that in his previous marriage, Carl had dragged his mother-in-law across their kitchen floor at least once. It was clear that Carl had been violent before.

Many evenings I heard Mom and Carl talking while I was in my bedroom for the night. Mom was pointing out to him that he shouldn't talk to me the way he did, that what he was doing was no way to treat a child.

Carl would listen to Mom, but never improved on how he treated me. He was always good to Mom, treating her respectfully. I could not figure out why he didn't treat me like that. But I realized that ever since I stopped kissing Daddy that disgusting way, he had never been the same. But I'd had to put a stop to his kisses; they felt wrong.

***

Things happened to me with other people, not always for my good.

The winter when I was eleven, Aunt Ann and Uncle John took me on a trip with them to Oregon over the weekend to visit Uncle John's brother and his family.

Aunt Ann drove that afternoon and evening, and Uncle John and I sat in the back seat. The night was cold, and Uncle John placed a blanket over our laps to keep us warm. I'd always liked Uncle John, but that weekend things happened to change my feelings toward him. Shortly after he placed the blanket on our laps, I felt Uncle John's hand within my underpants. His fingers were touching my body at places my mother told me never to let boys touch.

I wondered, what he's doing that for? I'd always trusted Uncle John before. What he is doing to me feels strange, but somehow it feels good. I don't think

43

he should be doing that. Mom told me one time not to let a boy touch me down there, or on my breasts.

This continued for a while, until we reached the family's home. I'd never been there before. It was a small, white, two-story house. I got to sleep in the bedroom with their eight-year-old daughter. Aunt Ann and Uncle John slept in another room. I was very happy about that. All during our stay in Oregon I tried to stay far away from Uncle John. I decided that what Uncle John had done on the way to Oregon was wrong. I was glad he didn't do anything else like that to me over the weekend or on the ride back to Seattle that Sunday evening.

Aunt Ann returned to work that Monday morning, leaving me with Uncle John, who worked evenings. I was to stay at their home with Uncle John that day, and go back to Kenniltown that night. Once Aunt Ann left, terrible things started to happen.

Uncle John was a very tall man. Later that morning, he came up to me in the living room, reached down and pulled me up to kiss me on my lips. I didn't know what to do, but decided I'd better let him kiss me. I was afraid of what he might do to me if I didn't.

That happened two or three more times that morning. Then it got worse. He said to me, "Liz, let's go in the bedroom. I can tell you want to do that with me, don't you?"

I didn't want to do that, but I was still afraid of him, so I let him take me into his and Aunt Ann's bedroom. Uncle John had me lie down on their bed. Then he lay on top of me. All of a sudden, something even stranger happened.

Why did Uncle John put that thing that men go to the bathroom with in-between my legs by where I go to the bathroom? That doesn't make any sense to me, I thought. I lay there, scared to death, with my head turned away from Uncle John. Finally, after what seemed a long time, he got off me, and we left the bedroom. Uncle John continued to kiss me a few more times that day. Finally, after what seemed like forever, Aunt Ann came home and drove me back to my home in Kenniltown. I was very glad to get away from Uncle John and be safe at home.

A few nights later, Mom, Daddy, and I were talking and Uncle John's name came up. I screamed, "I hate Uncle John!" Mom looked shocked and said, "Why do you feel that way now, Liz?"

"Because he touched me and did bad stuff in the places you told me never to let a man or boy touch me!"

"When did this happen?"

"Last week, on our way to Oregon, and when we were back at their house in Seattle."

My mother's face showed alarm and anger, "Well, we'll have to do something about that, Liz."

Later that evening, Daddy spoke to me. "Elizabeth, let's go for a walk together, you and me, and you can tell me all about what happened."

I didn't much trust Daddy either, so I said, "No, I don't want to do that!"

The next weekend we all went to Aunt Ann and Uncle John's small, beautiful home, overlooking Lake Washington, for dinner. Mom told her sister Ann what Uncle John had done to me. They both agreed they wouldn't say anything about the matter, because Uncle John would have to go to jail. They decided they would just be certain that Uncle John and I would never be left alone together again.

I'll just have to stay away from him, I thought, when I heard that. I sure hope he won't do anything like that to me anymore. Why did he do such strange things to me, anyway?

I spent that evening at Aunt Ann and Uncle John's house, hoping I could continue visiting there, as always. Mom did tell me that evening that I would not be able to go camping with them anymore. I had gone camping with them a couple times, so I felt sad about that. Mom, Carl, and I never did go camping, so now I wouldn't be able to go camping at all.

Since Mom and Aunt Ann decided not to say anything about what Uncle John did to me, I decided to forget all about the bad things he had done.

Most of the traumatic experiences I lived through, however, happened with Carl. Even though most of the episodes happened daily, other people didn't always understand what I was going through.

One of my girlfriends, Janet, didn't grasp why I disliked Carl. She said to me, "I don't see why you think your stepfather is so terrible, Liz. He doesn't seem bad to me. He's always pleasant when I talk to him."

Carl was at his best with people outside our family. As Janet spoke, I thought, if Carl were as nasty to her as he is to me, she'd have a very different opinion about him.

As time passed, I began to feel inferior to other young people. I didn't have that problem in Chicago, but these feelings started as Carl and I clashed so often. I had a few close friends that I talked to and told my feelings, but often in groups I didn't talk very much.

In our Camp Fire Girl troop, we took turns serving as president. When I was the last one elected president, I was devastated. Another time, I ran for class secretary at school. When I lost, I was so upset I cried. One of my girlfriends comforted me and told me that losing that election was not so awful, that I really shouldn't take it so seriously. To me, however, the defeat meant that I was not popular, and I wanted so much to be popular.

After learning I had lost the election, I was walking up the hill from downtown to our home. I thought, I'll show them, all the people who live here. I'll come back here one day, when I'm grown, and let them see what a success I am. Then they'll see my worth.

I also had some good experiences in Kenniltown, like weekends spent with Carol Wood and her family. Although they lived on a ranch outside of town, she still went to school with us. I had fun spending weekends with her, having napkins in napkin-rings at dinner, walking all over their ranch, petting her horses, and crossing their hanging bridge over their manmade lake. This time spent with her reminded me of what life was like in Chicago. I once told another girlfriend that my family back in Chicago was wealthy, but she replied, "Oh no, Liz, your family was not rich." That left me confused.

While in Kenniltown, I developed confusion about who I was. I was no longer a Scott. After all, wasn't I thousands of miles from Chicago? So, not being a Scott, I decided I must be a Jones. But the Jones's didn't have much money. In fact, Mom had to help Carl get out of debt when they married. I was used to being the granddaughter of a wealthy, refined doctor. I went from feeling rich with Grandoo in Chicago, to going without money for after-school snacks in Kenniltown.

One of the good things going on in my life then was my relationship with Carl's parents. I did love Carl's mother and father. They were not like him; they were very kind and loving to me. I loved to play Canasta with Grandpa. In the beginning, he'd always beat me, but later I started beating him part of the time. I would also help Grandma with the dishes, and we would talk. I couldn't figure out how such nice parents had a son like Carl, who was mean and full of hatred.

Since most of my clothes were old and mended, I looked into the possibilities of earning some money to buy new clothes. I learned I could get a job because I was twelve years old, picking blueberries each August. Carl said he could take me to the blueberry patch on his way to work in the mornings and pick me up on his way back at night.

My blueberry-picking day began at 5:30 a.m., with the ring of my alarm clock. I ate breakfast and rode the ten miles to the blueberry patch. The part of these summer days that I hated most were the rides back home with Carl. I hated facing his glassy stare. Riding with him was anything but pleasant. Even if he was quiet, his eyes looked wild. I did make it through the summer, however, earning one hundred dollars, twenty of which was an award I received for good attendance.

Later, I asked Mom if I could take more dancing lessons than just the two a week I had been taking. By this time, I was also taking piano lessons once a week. Mom said she couldn't afford to pay for more dancing lessons for me. She suggested that perhaps my teacher, Cheryl Howard, could use some help at the studio that would cover the cost of more lessons.

We talked to Cheryl, and she told us that she could use some help with her bookkeeping. She said that she'd consider hiring me to do the bookkeeping in exchange for lessons. From then on, every Wednesday afternoon and evening, and all day Saturday, I was at the studio either working or taking lessons. I loved doing both. I made coffee first thing in the mornings for Cheryl and her pianist, and then I proudly took my place at the desk to check in the students, taking in money for lessons and other purchases from their parents. Cheryl's mother, an accountant, trained me for my bookkeeping responsibilities.

I enjoyed talking to the different parents while working. They all said I must be bright, as I was a young girl doing the bookkeeping. Cheryl used to say that, too. She'd tell me that she didn't understand the bookkeeping, but she sure was glad I did.

There was another dancing student, Judy Straight, who took lessons with me. She was also Cheryl's assistant teacher. Judy danced so well. Originally, her parents started her lessons in order to improve her health, and for that reason, she had taken several lessons each week from a very young age. I was in awe of her ability. She had such control of her body and did such beautiful and difficult things with it.

As we grew older, Judy and I worked together; I was always very jealous of her. I remember disliking her because I could not dance as well as she could, so these feelings would always cloud our relationship. For her part, Judy was always nice to me and would often wink and smile at me in friendship. All I could think of was that she was a better dancer than I.

During these years, in the 50s, I was taking many lessons, and I also danced often in amateur events. When I was fifteen, I tried out and was accepted by an amateur entertainment troupe in Seattle. I danced solo routines, performing at some military bases, as well as for many other audiences, like Boy Scout special programs and TV shows. I performed a tap dance routine to the song, "Rock Around the Clock," which was broadcast on television all throughout Seattle.

I also did a modern jazz dance to "One Mint Julep," a song that had been banned because of sexual taboos at the time. I wore a black satin costume with a blue satin lining and sequins, which I designed.

I really loved dancing, and my goal was to become a professional dancer. I told Karen, another friend, I wanted to become a better dancer than Judy. She replied, "Liz, you know, no matter how good a dancer you become, there'll always be someone better. That's just the way life is." This was discouraging for me to think about.

These were days full of activities and happy times, but they also continued to be hellish days with Carl, as he continued to condemn me.

Going to church helped some. Most Sundays I attended the Congregational Church in Kenniltown. It was just a few blocks from our home, so I walked there and back on Sundays.

There was a Baptist Church near our home, but my friends all went to the Congregational Church, so I chose to go there. Sometimes, when I walked past the Baptist Church, I heard what seemed to me to be strange music. It was different from the music at our church, and it made me wonder what it meant.

A song that I loved to sing at church was, "Oh, Love That Will Not Let Me Go." I would think about coming from God before I was born, and how those

53

words must have meant that God wanted to keep me all my life. I loved thinking that.

When I was ten, Mom arranged for my baptism. In the Congregational Church, baptism is by sprinkling. I felt a little strange that day because I was ten years old, and most children are baptized when they are babies. I didn't feel any different after my baptism.

Mom and Carl didn't go to church. Mom was too tired from working five and a half days a week, taking care of me, Carl, the house, and worrying about the problems in our family. Carl did not believe in going to church and would tell me, "The church is not going to pay your bills for you, you know." I wanted to go to church, anyway, so I did and I usually also went to Sunday School.

I would sit in church and listen to Easter sermons and other sermons and wonder how all the Christianity business related to me. I heard of Jesus Christ's resurrection and thought, but how does that affect me? I couldn't figure out how whatever I learned in church had any effect on me or my life.

One of the things I did like about the Congregational Church was spending time on retreats in the Cascade Mountains. Sometimes in the winter we'd stay in a cabin and go hiking on the snow-filled trails. We'd sometimes see cougar tracks, but we never saw a cougar. We had warm fellowship on these retreats and I had fun, but I still couldn't understand what the church had to do with my life.

One weekend on retreat, our minister and I discussed, for the first time, the way Carl talked to me and how his words made me feel. The minister said it was amazing to him how well my personality had turned out, considering the ordeal I was going through.

I continued to turn the other cheek to Carl, but, beneath the surface, a real storm brewed within me. I had many repressed emotions and feelings in response to Carl—feelings that I wouldn't express to him or even think about.

We also had Sunday evening youth group fellowship meetings. I believed that the young people and adults were "too good," and "too square." Life had so many exciting things in it, most of them not condoned by the church. It seemed to me the church was too rigid, and they expected too much from young people.

I also had some other religious experiences while living in Kenniltown. I lay in bed one summer, recovering from a tonsillectomy, and read *The Greatest*

Book Ever Written and *The Greatest Story Ever Told*. These books about the Old and New Testaments in the Bible told of personal experiences the patriarchs and saints had with God. I thought, wouldn't it be wonderful to talk to God the way these men and women did? I'd love to have an experience like Moses had with the burning bush.

Television stars Dale Evens and Roy Rogers seemed to be strong Christians, as well. I watched them on television while they testified that they knew Jesus Christ personally. I thought that was rather unusual, because I had never heard that at church. How could we "know" Jesus Christ? I found that interesting but didn't understand it. I wondered if this could this be an answer to understanding what Christianity means to us.

One day a woman who lived next door, whom I'd never met, knocked on our door and asked me if I'd ever accepted Jesus as my personal Savior. I don't remember my reply. It was probably about my already going to church. Again I thought, what does that mean?

Aunt Martha, Grandma Jones' sister, visited us often. She spoke of God's grace and love for us in sending His Son to bring us into a relationship with God through Christ's death on the cross. Although I knew Aunt Martha's faith was like the other testimonies I'd heard, her belief in God didn't seem strange to me. She was so loving and kind. She had been in a psychiatric hospital once. Grandma said Aunt Martha's husband tricked her into going there. I never could see anything about Aunt Martha that seemed like mental illness.

The grown daughter of the family next door also had been a psychiatric patient. When I saw her outside I thought, how is she mentally ill? She seems just like everybody else. What does it mean to be mentally ill?

Mental illness fascinated me, especially a condition called "schizophrenia." After talking to Aunt Ann about this condition, I wrote a paper for school on which I received an A+, and I memorized how to spell the word schizophrenia.

Despite Carl's behavior, good things also happened to me in Kenniltown. Almost every summer I went camping with our Camp Fire Girls' Troop. We had a lot of good times, hunting for driftwood, cooking over campfires, and hiking. But I still felt unpopular, not as well liked as the other girls, and I also experienced feelings of loneliness and wondered why I didn't consider life fulfilling.

There were times I wished we could leave Kenniltown and start over fresh, with a newer, more modern home, new friends, and a new church. My chance to move came after my sophomore year in high school; Carl took a new Civil Service job in Briceville, a town across the Cascade Mountains in Eastern Washington.

Carl worked for the federal government, working with the Army Engineers in Seattle for twelve years. He felt that people there were after him and that his job wasn't secure. He resented others who were promoted over him, even though they hadn't been with the government as long. He wanted to transfer to a job somewhere else. He was able to do that, so we left Kenniltown for Briceville.

When I told Karen we were moving to Central Washington, her comment was, "Oh, Liz! You won't like that part of the state nearly as much as here. It's mainly desert and lacks the greenery of Seattle. I bet you'll wish you hadn't moved." However, I found Briceville a nice town. It had a population of forty thousand, making it significantly bigger than Kenniltown.

We didn't sell our little house in Kenniltown, but traded it for a down payment on a new home in Briceville. The new house was custom-built and much larger than our bungalow in Kenniltown. The house was tri-level, with three bedrooms, one and a half baths, living room, dining room, kitchen, garage, and a recreation room, which became my dance studio. The master bedroom was the size of many living rooms. It was a new house, located on the outskirts of town, with a peach orchard blossoming directly behind our back yard.

Dancing lessons continued in Briceville. One of my teachers was a young woman who had danced on Broadway. We did some great Modern Jazz routines with her. One day, I stopped off at another studio, St Vincent's School of Dance. I watched some classes from their viewing room. I registered at St Vincent's for ballet. I continued with tap and Modern Jazz at the first studio.

One day I told some of the girls at the downtown studio what a fantastic ballet teacher Mrs. St. Vincent was. When the owner of the studio heard, he told me

I could not take lessons from two studios at the same time. I chose St. Vincent's and ballet. My best friend in Briceville, Betty Carter, continued to take lessons at the downtown studio. When I went with her to their spring recital, the owner refused to allow me in. I thought that was a high price to pay for my "sin."

Mr. and Mrs. St. Vincent were dear friends. I believe they were French. They taught me strict ballet, suitable for ballerinas in the ballet companies. I had to relearn ballet, keep my hips in place, and learn correct "placement."

I was also on the Teen-Age Club of Briceville (TACB) Council. The YMCA sponsored the council, and each grade in high school selected a boy and a girl representative. I was the female member from the eleventh grade.

We had a great time in TACB. Every Friday night we had a dance with a live band of local high school students. One fellow played the saxophone so well that I asked him to play "One Mint Julep" for my dance. As well as dancing Jazz, I also occasionally danced a Hawaiian Hula or a Tap dance.

In Briceville, I felt more popular than I had in Kenniltown. In spite of Karen's prediction, I ended up liking Briceville better than Kenniltown.

I attended a Congregational Church in Briceville. I still wondered about Christianity's ultimate meaning.

After moving to Briceville, occasionally Mom, Carl, and I went to church together. The church was several miles from our home, but we had a car now. Going to church didn't change Carl's behavior any. When I rode home from church with Mom and Carl, I often felt worse than before going to church. Why should church affect me like that? I wondered. It didn't make any sense. Church is supposed to lift us up, not let us down.

The youth group in our town's church had many activities, including Sunday evening fellowship. The young people were nice to me, and I felt accepted. Still I wondered why my friends enjoyed church activities so much. Didn't they miss all the exciting parts of life that were not condoned by the church? What about necking and petting with a boy on a date? It seemed too strict to believe that we can do nothing sexual until we get married.

I had found out the how babies are conceived by men and women a year earlier, when a girlfriend told me. Mom had never told me, nor had I received any education about sex. At the time, the process involved seemed strange to me. I had experienced some of the same sexual activities on dates that Uncle John had done with me in the back seat of his car years earlier. I wondered why men always seemed to do those kinds of things. I decided those experiences must be somehow involved in the whole process of sexual interaction. But I knew that the church said that those behaviors were sinful. I continued to wonder about lots of issues regarding how the church said I should live my life. After a while, I stopped attending the Sunday night youth group meetings.

Our school had a talent show that spring. My "One Mint Julep" dance took third place. I was the only dancer to place in the show. Before we had the talent show, we had rehearsals. One evening Carl drove my friend Betty and me to and from the rehearsal. Coming home, Carl met us with all kinds of accusations. He claimed he had seen us in a car with men "carrying on." He even claimed the men were strangers, not our teenage friends.

Since that incident, Betty was afraid to get in the same car with Carl. She told me she'd had no idea he could be so vicious. To me, Carl's behavior was just the usual. Still, I could understand Betty's fear because she usually didn't see this side of Carl. When I arrived home, I assured Mom that Carl's newest accusations were either a lie or the product of his imagination. He had continued all through the years to accuse and condemn me and to tell me I was "no good."

In Briceville, I smoked my first and only cigarette. A girlfriend of mine, older than I, kept insisting I try smoking. One night we went into the orchards behind the house and lit up. I didn't inhale, but I liked that cigarette. It helped me relax and feel good. I decided that since I didn't get an allowance, I'd never have the money to buy cigarettes, and I might like smoking so much I would have a hard time quitting. I decided that even though smoking was popular, it was not for me.

The summer after my junior year, I worked at an A&W Root Beer Stand as a carhop. That's where I met Bill Peterson. He was older than I was. When he pulled unto the A&W, we started talking while I waited on him. After flirting with me for a while, we continued to talk, and he told me he was divorced.

One afternoon Bill asked if I'd like to go out with him. Excitedly I replied, "Sure, Bill!"

We went to a drive-in movie. Bill said, "I've been looking for a really sweet girl to date, and I think you're that girl." This brought a smile to my face and made me feel special.

That was the summer of 1957. Mom and Carl took a trip to California. Carl wanted to check out the job situation there, because he started having the same feelings of persecution in Briceville that he had in Kenniltown. Again, he was looking for a change of employment within civil service. Most of those two weeks my parents were out of town I spent with Bill, either at my home or other places. I decided that with Bill as my boyfriend, I wanted to find out what it was like to experience sex "all the way." The Bible refers to sexual intercourse as a man and woman "knowing" each other. So, Bill and I began to "know" each other.

I knew from the Bible that I was only supposed to have sex if I was married, but I rationalized that Bill and I would get married, so it was not sinful. I did like the experience, and we repeated it several times.

One night Bill confided in me that he had been in jail once or twice. After hearing that, I said to my friend Betty, "Gosh, It's really exciting having a boy-friend who's been in jail! Maybe I can help him. I've always had in the back of my mind the thought that I'd like to go with a guy who's been in trouble."

One day while I was working at the A&W, a fellow I didn't know, but who knew Bill, told me, "You know, Liz, Bill's not divorced. He's married and has children. He's telling you he's divorced, but it's a lie."

I had a naïve, trusting faith in Bill. I replied, "If Bill tells me he's divorced, then as far as I'm concerned, he is divorced. It's as simple as that."

Shortly after Mom and Carl returned from California, Grandma and Grandpa Jones came from Kenniltown. While visiting, my grandparents found out about Bill and me. They heard that he was married, and they believed it.

One evening Mom said to me, "I'm sorry, Liz, but Bill is too old for you. It's also rumored that he's married. I'm going to have to forbid you to see him anymore."

I wasn't used to Mom giving me ultimatums, and I was not about to stop seeing Bill. That evening, I waited until very late when everyone else was asleep.

I took my trusty dancing case with my dancing shoes, leotard, and a new expensive book I had about ballet. I started walking from my side of town across to Bill's home. Around 4:30 a.m., I arrived outside Bill and his mother's place. I didn't want to wake anyone, so I slipped into his unlocked car and fell asleep.

"All right, get out of there, young lady!" It was the voice of a police officer. He yanked me out of the car. Carl and his father had asked the police officer to come after me with them. They suspected I'd gone to Bill's home in defiance. Evidently, they involved the police because they didn't want to come after me alone.

On the way home from Bill's, Carl and his father kept yelling at me, "You're going to have to go to reform school!" I found it hard to believe I'd be put in reform school for running away from home and sleeping in a car. But that's what they kept insisting.

Mom was upset because I ran away. But her tactics were quite different from Carl's. She simply told me I could not see Bill, but that if I obeyed, everything would be fine. She said I was definitely not going to reform school, no matter what Carl and his father said.

Life went on, without Bill.

Chapter Five

CALIFORNIA CONVERSION

Lancaster, 1957

I was sad when we left Briceville, but I believed California was a great place to live if I wanted a career as a professional dancer. Carl was hired as a civil service employee in Palmdale, located in the Mojave Desert. We would live in Lancaster, nearby.

I learned that Bill had also moved to California. I wanted to get in touch with him there, as I wasn't able to forget about him. We'd had a sexual relationship that I wanted to continue. I wanted to avoid sinning that way with another man. I decided marrying Bill would be the answer to this problem. Unable to contact him, my life went on.

I remember my first impressions of California. Everywhere we went there was desert, and it was terribly hot. For the first time I saw tumbleweed, and it looked exactly like it did in the movies. It was quite a contrast to Washington State, especially compared to the greenery in Seattle.

We temporarily stayed at a large motel. The first night, I walked up to the lobby to look at magazines and see what was happening. I noticed two men watching TV; one of them was unbelievably handsome. He was easily as handsome as any movie star.

"Hi, how are you tonight?" the good-looking man said to me. You mean he's actually talking to me? I thought. I noticed he had a nice voice, as well.

"I'm fine, thanks," I replied. "What's going on tonight? I was getting bored, just sitting in my room."

"We were bored, too! Are you vacationing here in town?" This new friend seemed interested in me.

"No, we're going to live here. We're looking for an apartment and just staying here temporarily." After talking for a few minutes, the good-looking man introduced himself. "I'm Mario Martino. What's your name?"

"Liz Jones," I replied.

"Well, Liz, would you like to go for a swim with me tomorrow in the pool? We could get to know each other better."

"Sure, I'd like to go for a swim! What time?"

"Since tomorrow is Saturday, and I don't have to work, how about going in the morning about ten. That'll give us both a chance to sleep in."

"Fine, that sounds like a wonderful idea, Mario. I'll see you tomorrow.

Good night."

Walking back to our room, I couldn't help but think about Mario, one of the best-looking men I'd ever met. Bill was not nearly as handsome, but he was still my special someone. It seemed to me that no matter how good looking a man I would meet, he wouldn't be able to take the place of Bill.

Mario and I spent a lot of time together that fall. Mom, Carl, and I left the motel and moved into an apartment in Lancaster. Mario worked for a large aircraft company in St. Louis and was temporarily in California while working in the space program. He often took me out to dinner; we would eat at nice restaurants two or three times a week.

Mario and I often talked about Bill and me. He spoke to me in a brotherly way, assuring me that I would find another man who would take Bill's place, even though it didn't seem possible at that time.

I was still trying to locate Bill in California. However, I was able to learn his phone number. I called, and his father answered. When I asked for Bill he said, "Bill's not here, but I can ask his wife when he'll be back." I told him not to bother, and hung up. Darn, I thought, he really is married! I can't marry him, after all.

Then there was Mario. He told me more than once he wanted to have sex with me. I'd told him about the relationship I had with Bill. I didn't want to have sex with Mario because I believed that would be sinful. I had learned enough about Christianity to know what the Bible teaches about sexual relationships. It says sex should only be between one man and one woman for life. Mario would be my second man.

Then, one night when Mario and I were in the car, I finally gave in, and we had sex. Right afterward, I felt terribly guilty. I looked up at the heavens and thought, now I've really sinned. When I die, I'll go to hell. But regardless of my thoughts, I continued this behavior for the remainder of Mario's stay in California.

One night, after Mario and I had dated for two months, we sat in his room at the motel, and he told me he had to leave soon for St. Louis. He looked at me and asked, "Liz, would you like to go back to St. Louis with me and get married?"

Right away I thought, I'm only sixteen. So I responded, "I'm too young to get married, Mario. I haven't even finished high school. Anyway, I want to become a professional dancer."

Although Mario's proposal thrilled me, I couldn't conceive of quitting high school and going to St. Louis. I said, "I'm sorry. I just don't think I can even consider marriage right now."

A few days later Mario left for St. Louis. I had mixed feelings. I knew I'd miss him, but I also knew that he was considerably older than I. He told me he was twenty-eight, and he had a son from his first marriage. Mario told me that his first wife died giving birth to their son, who was four years old. Mario was raising him alone.

So, I had no boyfriend. Bill was married, and Mario was gone. I felt very bad about how I had behaved with both of them. When I got into our bathtub to bathe, I felt so dirty. I found myself thinking, this is terrible. If I keep participating in these affairs, I'll probably end up a whore. That would be so dreadful. God must really be mad at me.

I need to start going to church again, I thought. I wonder if there is a Congregational Church here. I couldn't find that denomination in Lancaster. Eating lunch one day in the school cafeteria with some other students, one of the girls overheard me say that my church didn't have a congregation there. She spoke to me and said, "Liz, why don't you visit my church? We'd love to have you!"

"What church do you attend?"

"The First Baptist Church, right down the street from here."

That Sunday, Mom and I visited my friend's church. Quite different from the Congregational Church, this Baptist Church presented answers to my questions like, how does Christianity affect me personally?

"No matter how much you have sinned before God, no matter what evil acts you've done in public or in private, God has provided a "way out" for you and me, a way for us to avoid punishment for our sins. Jesus Christ died for your sins and mine, and all we have to do is turn away from our sins, accept what He's done for us, and simply receive this gift of salvation by accepting Jesus Christ as Lord and Savior."

The minister stressed the positive aspect of the Christian Gospel. Although he spoke of our sinful conditions and our lack of perfection, he stressed the saving power of God's love toward us in Jesus Christ, His death on the cross, and His resurrection.

I'd never heard the gospel explained. All those years before, I sat in church in Kenniltown and Briceville wondering, what is the meaning of Christianity? What is its power for humans? Now this Baptist minister provided me with the answers.

"So, if you would like to receive this free gift from God, I'd like you to make your decision public by walking down the aisle right now. After that, we'll counsel with you about the power available to you from Christ."

Wow, I thought, my sins can be forgiven if I turn away from my sinful life and accept Jesus and what He did for me when He died on the cross. Maybe I should go ahead and walk down the aisle as the minister said. Well, maybe not yet.

The next Sunday morning, Mom and I went back to the Baptist church. That evening in the service, I went forward and accepted Christ. I felt overwhelming relief as God lifted the penalty of every sin

I'd ever committed and ever would commit from my soul. This was the most earth-shaking event of my life. I was experiencing a spiritual rebirth; I was "born again." For the first time, I was starting to know God the same way the great men in the Bible knew Him.

The first time I told Carl and Mom about my conversion, they were shocked, especially Carl. I said some unusual statements that first night. I sat at our dining table in the apartment in Lancaster, and told Mom and Carl, "It's great to be a true Christian! I'm so happy, I could run out in the street and announce to everyone, 'I've been saved! Praise the Lord!'"

I'm sure Carl thought, Elizabeth is really crazy now. He'd often told me, through the years, "You're crazy. You're really crazy, Elizabeth!"

A week or so later, I asked some of the senior members of my new church questions about how I should react to my stepfather and the way he treated me. "You should turn your other cheek, Liz," one of the ladies told me.

When she said that, I wondered about it, because a month before I became a Christian, I'd gotten very mad at Carl and yelled at him for the first time. I'd pounded my fist on the floor of our apartment's living room. But now, as a Christian, for better or for worse, I continued on turning my other cheek to Carl.

On Wednesday evenings we had prayer meetings at church. Youth fellowship was on Sunday evenings, and later, the evening service. We'd stand up and testify about our faith. I'd briefly tell the story of my life and my sins, testifying of God's forgiveness and my salvation. I felt healed and whole.

Sometimes our pastor's sermons were about Bible prophesy. He would say, "We're living in very trying times when prophesies are coming to pass. The rapture could happen at any time. Jesus will return as He said He would, and no one but God the Father knows when He'll come. Believers will meet Him in the air and be with Him forever."

He also told us that every believer's name is written by God in the "Lamb's Book of Life" in heaven, and their names are never out of that book. I considered myself very fortunate to be a Christian.

After this, and for the remainder of that year, church became the focal point of my social life. I found the high-school-age members, as well as the other members, very warm, friendly, and accepting. The fun we had was clean fun, and I understood then how a person could enjoy wholesome activities. I no longer questioned the attractiveness of the straight Christian life.

Now that I had a personal closeness with God, I felt a brotherhood and sisterhood in Christ with my friends at this Baptist Church. We were all members of the family of God. With this new faith and love, jealously seldom entered my heart. Hadn't Christ commanded us to love our neighbors as we love ourselves? I was discovering that love was a nicer emotion to have in my heart than the jealousy and hatred I felt before.

School went on, but the focus was changing. Now I had so many friends at church for which I felt only love. I had grown to the point where I loved my brothers and sisters in Christ and loved my fellowship with them. This was quite new to me, and it was delightful. More time would be needed for me to also feel the same love for everyone.

By the time I started my senior year in Lancaster, I had completed most of my required high school subjects. I really had a good time in school, making all A's that year.

Biology was fun. We studied evolution, and I wrote a special report on Darwin's theories. Naturally, being a Bible-believing Christian, I didn't accept the theory of evolution. My teacher and I discussed this issue often. One day the teacher said to me, as he tried to convince me that man had evolved, "Liz, if you can go to college, major in biology, graduate, and then you still accept the creation account in Genesis as literal fact, I'll have another talk with you and be amazed." The same teacher really surprised me at the end of the year when he awarded me the Senior Class Award in Science, anti-evolution and all.

While all these events were happening, I was trying to get Mom to "go forward" in church. I was convinced that she was not really a true Christian. I had gone forward, and now I knew I was saved. Mother had never "gone forward," so by definition she was not a Christian.

I was ardent in my attempts. She knew she was a Christian, I'm sure, that she had been one since her youth, with her Christian family and her Methodist upbringing. But she did go forward, partly to please me. She was also baptized by immersion, as I had been after my conversion. My baptism in the water in the front section of the church was quite meaningful. Even though I'd been baptized by sprinkling as a child, Baptists believe in baptism by full immersion after one accepts Christ.

The concept of dying to sin and being raised again to a new life in Christ was very significant to me as I was baptized in the church. Perhaps it was meaningful to Mom, as well, when she had the same experience.

Since I was trying to live the Christian life, and our new church didn't believe in numerous worldly activities, I could no longer dance. Dancing was regarded as sinful. Since it was not considered acceptable, I no longer danced. I had a difficult time coming to this decision. It was hard for me to understand why, just because I'd found the gospel and become a Christian, I could no longer dance, when dancing was such a large part of my life. I decided that this sacrifice was necessary. Of course, our church didn't believe in smoking or drinking. I was glad I'd never got into any of those vices.

That year I had several boyfriends. I had new feelings regarding dating, however. I wanted to stop completely participating in any sexual or pre-sexual activities because of my new faith. A fellow named

Al and I "went steady" for quite a while that year. He lived across the street from us with two other fellows, who were all out of school and working. I never felt I was in love with Al, but I really liked him. I was quite attracted to Greg, one of Al's roommates. He was a good-looking guy, and very nice. But he was usually going with one girl or another, and I was Al's steady girlfriend.

At the end of the school year, a group of us went up in the mountains to have an all-night party at a cabin. By then, I was in the process of breaking up with Al. I went to the party with Greg, and Al went with one of Greg's former girlfriends. The four of us drove up together, Greg and me in the front seat, and Al and the other girl in the back. We had a good time in the mountains. About 4 a.m. Saturday morning, Greg and I innocently fell asleep on the sofa-bed next to each other. We must have slept until 10 a.m. or so. When we got up, we all had breakfast. Al's date was quite upset about Greg's and my "night" together, insisting we made love. I told her that we hadn't, though I don't think she believed me.

I enjoyed being liked by the boys and dating so much. I liked the new "abundant life" Christ spoke of when He said, "I am come that you might have life, and that you might have it more abundantly." The loving Spirit which filled me not only made me happier, but evidently it made me more attractive to others as well.

Unfortunately, I was quite attractive to Carl, also. He decided I needed to learn about sex—from him. We'd moved to a house from our apartment. One day he said, "Elizabeth, it's time that you learn about the facts of life. I don't want you to tell your mother we're discussing this. I don't want to her to know.

"Here are some magazines," he continued, "that will help you learn about the things men and women do when they make love." He handed me the magazines, which appeared to be pornographic. Repulsed by them, I refused to look through the dirty magazines.

"And," Carl went on, "I want to give you this." He handed me a cylindrically shaped object about six inches long and one inch wide.

"What's this for?" I asked Carl.

"That's for you to use to break your hymen," he answered. "You should do that soon. I'll talk to you more about that later. For now just put the magazines and that under your rug so your mother won't find them. Remember, don't tell her about this."

I wondered, why doesn't he want me to tell Mom about our discussion? Maybe he won't bring it up again. I hope not.

The next day, Carl approached me again and said, "Elizabeth, I want to talk to you. I want to tell you more about men and women and their sex lives. Most of the time a man stimulates the woman quite a bit before actual intercourse takes place. I try to excite your mother quite a bit at first, myself."

As Carl continued, I couldn't help but wish I could get away from him and this conversation. I made a mental decision to tell Mom about these episodes and stop them before anything frightening happened. The next day I told Mom what had been going on. She soon ended the matter by confronting Carl and telling him the sessions had to stop. As I expected, Carl was more unpleasant to me than usual after Mom's talk with him.

After all this happened with Carl, I decided to tell Mom, for the first time, that in Briceville I'd lost my virginity. Mom had never taught me about sex. She'd only told me not to let any man touch me on my genitals or my breasts. I found out everything for myself. What I'd picked up about God's laws regarding sex was from Sunday School and church as a child.

Mom and I met to talk in my bedroom. Carl wasn't home. "Mom, I need to tell you about something"

"Okay."

"Carl, as you know, wanted to teach me about sex. But, I need to tell you that I already have had sexual relationships, both with Bill in Briceville, and here in Lancaster with Mario. Right after becoming a Christian, I stopped participating in any kind of sexual activities. That's why I was so happy to hear about forgiveness from the Lord Jesus."

"Liz," Mom said, "I need to tell you about something, also. Your father Kenneth and I were not married when I became pregnant with you. I was thirty-two years old and a virgin. My parents had passed way when I met your father. He was a very handsome lawyer, and he belonged to a very prestigious family in Chicago. We dated, and he expressed sexual interest in me. I had been brought up by Christian parents and never done anything like that. My girlfriends at the Methodist church I attended told me they were having sexual relationships with their boyfriends. It seemed to be the latest trend. So, I eventually gave in. I knew nothing about sex, but Kenneth told me that if I showered afterwards, I wouldn't get pregnant. We dated for a year, or so, and Kenneth assured me we would get married. But, then, when I became pregnant, Kenneth wanted me to have an abortion. You know, Liz, my father had been a doctor who never believed in abortion. When I wouldn't agree to have the abortion, Kenneth told me that would be the only way we could continue our relationship. So, our dating relationship ended.

"My brother Gerald decided to take me to meet Kenneth's father, your grandfather, Dr Jonathan Scott. Your beloved Grandoo took over the situation right away and helped me tremendously from then on. He was such a wonderful man! When I started showing in my pregnancy, Dr. Scott found a nice home for women who were in my situation. After you were born, he supported us in an apartment. Your grandfather tried very hard for a long time to get his son to do the right thing and marry me. But Kenneth wouldn't budge. He wouldn't even come to his father's home. Eventually, before you were born, Dr Scott finally convinced

Kenneth to marry me for the purpose of giving you your name, Elizabeth Scott, so you wouldn't be illegitimate. I had to promise to give Kenneth a divorce right after your birth."

"That must have been very hard for you, Mom! But, when did we go to live with Grandoo at his home?"

"When you were about one year old."

"It's no wonder you weren't very happy at Grandoo's with all the Scott family."

"You're right, but your grandfather was always wonderful to both of us. He told me I was his favorite daughter-in-law, and you were his favorite grandchild!"

Mom continued and said, "I'm glad you now know about all of this, Liz. I wouldn't want you to learn these facts from someone else. Also, as I believe I've told you before, I was warned about your father by a good friend of your grandparents in Chicago. Mrs. Stone told me that I shouldn't let you around Kenneth, because he would 'ruin' you; he might sexually abuse you. She had a summer home in France. Kenneth would stay with her there. She said he did things while there which were so harmful, she believed that he would take advantage of you if he had the chance. That's why I've always been against you meeting him. Of course he never came to see us, anyway."

"Yes, you did tell me about Father, Mom. But I didn't know about your getting pregnant before you were married. You always said you were divorced. I appreciate your telling me."

After learning the details of my birth, I understood many things better, and I tucked the new knowledge in my heart to carry with me.

As the end of the school year was approaching, Pete, a friend from church, invited me and a girlfriend to his family's home for dinner. After we finished eating, Pete said he wanted to show us some of his books. Pointing to a couple of them on a shelf he said, "These books have supernatural powers. If you look at certain pictures, you will become demon-possessed."

"You've got to be kidding, Pete. No book has that kind of power. I'll show you. Let me look at one of those pictures."

"All right, Liz."

I looked at a picture, and said, "See, I looked right at a picture and nothing happened. I'll never be demon possessed! Anyway, I don't believe in demons."

I didn't notice any changes in my feelings or emotions, so I decided that whoever had concocted that idea about the pictures must have been wrong.

The Homecoming Queen of our Antelope Valley Joint Union High School class wrote in my yearbook, "Liz, you are one of the sweetest girls I have ever known. I wish I could have gotten to know you better. I don't know what you are going to do next year, but I hope you will have all the luck and happiness you deserve, and that's a lot!"

She was right in stating we didn't know each other well. When I read what she wrote, I felt warm all over because she was so beautiful and popular. She had such kind words about me; I thought, maybe I am popular after all. What did the next year hold for me? What college would I attend? I had been working on those decisions for a couple of months.

Chapter Six

UNHEALTHY BELIEVER

Los Angeles, 1958

Rev. Henry Compton, our church's Christian Education Minister, took several of us high school seniors to visit two Bible colleges. The first school we visited had a beautiful campus on a hill overlooking the Pacific Ocean. When I learned the cost of tuition, room, and board, I realized there was no way I would be able to afford that school.

I was going to have to work my way through college, because Carl had lost his government job, and Mom was supporting us. I'd received an inheritance at age thirteen when Grandoo died. Since I was a minor, my mother managed my inheritance, but now we had to use those funds to pay our bills.

The second college we visited with Henry was L.A. Trinity Bible College. When I first saw L.A.

Trinity, I noticed that it was not as beautiful as the school we'd just visited, but my thought was, maybe it won't be as expensive.

Two girls came off the elevator and greeted us with big smiles, saying, "Hi! How are you?"

I replied, "Fine. We're considering coming to this school in the fall.

How do you like it here?"

"It's really a great school! Everyone's so friendly, and the Christian fellowship is wonderful. I know if you decide to come here, you won't be sorry."

I was impressed with the friendliness of these girls. They seemed happy, enthusiastic, and they exuded warm, positive energy. This must be an exciting school to attend, I decided. When I inquired about the tuition, room, and board, I learned that if I worked twenty hours a week, I could afford to pay my way through school. I would need to fill out forms, arrange to work in some department of the college, and return for interviews before fall.

As we were leaving the college campus, I thought back to our encounter with the two friendly girls, and how, working part-time, I would be able to afford to attend this college. I decided L.A. Trinity Bible

College was the one for me. I believed the Lord must have been leading me to make this decision. This school definitely had the right Spirit.

With the new school year approaching, I needed to buy new clothes, so I decided to get a summer job. I couldn't ask Mom for any money for clothes, since finances were tight. One Friday evening in Lancaster, I was looking at clothes in a small, local dress shop when the owner approached me and asked how I liked his selection. I replied, "You've really got some nice clothes. I wish I could buy something. If I can find a summer job, I'll come back."

"Why don't you work for me?" He asked. "I can use some help this summer. If you work here, we'll give you a twenty-percent discount on any clothes you buy."

"That sounds great!" I was already calculating how many different dresses, skirts and sweaters I'd be able to buy.

"I've worked before," I added. "Last summer I was a car hop at an A & W Root Beer Stand. I've also done babysitting, worked in various berry fields, and done bookkeeping in a dancing school."

"Then you probably won't have any trouble learning what you need to know here. We can teach you how to use the cash register in no time."

Happily, I accepted his offer and started working the next week. I enjoyed working at the dress shop and worked six days a week. Lancaster was very hot in the summer. I walked to work in the mornings, wondering if anywhere else on earth could be as unbearable as the Mojave Desert in the summer.

I had never worked so many hours each week. Every single day I would be up early, walking either to my job or to church. I couldn't find any time to relax, and I became weary and exhausted. Soon I was yearning for the summer to end and my job to be over, even though I loved the Thompsons and their store.

We left Lancaster the beginning of August. Carl was not able to find another government job. He and Mom decided to accept a job at a hotel in Hollywood, which they would manage, and in return would have a small apartment.

For the first three weeks in Hollywood, I was utterly exhausted. I would sleep until 2:00 or 3:00 in the afternoon, get up and do a few things around the apartment or go for a walk, then go to bed early and sleep late the next day. When I thought about possible reasons for my exhaustion, all I could think of was the fact that I'd worked very hard this summer as well as being very active in church. I was a little puzzled, because I believed that most people work and go to church, so why did it bother me so much? Why was I so tired? I hoped I'd be rested in time for school.

When school started, I was assigned to the Mailing Department at Trinity. My main task was running the multigraph machine, somewhat of a cross between a mimeograph and a printing machine. I worked with a fellow named Ben, who'd worked there the previous year.

I liked the other students from the beginning. This was the first time I'd lived away from home, and it was starting out to be a good experience. I had lots of friends, and a great roommate. My schedule was very busy. I got up at 5:30 in the morning and went to breakfast. My first class began at 7:30, and classes continued straight through until lunch. After lunch, I went to work until 5:00 p.m. In the evenings, I studied until at least 11:00 p.m. Obviously, I got very little sleep. I averaged five hours sleep a night. I often felt like a sleepwalker early in the morning.

Smog was terrible at Trinity's downtown campus. In the middle of the day it was at its worst, and I often read though teary eyes.

My favorite class that year was Bible—Old Testament Studies. We took four semester hours of Old Testament Studies both semesters. I also took a course in memorizing lots of Bible verses, two Christian Education courses, World History, Physical Science, English, and Introduction to Fine Arts.

I had a hard time deciding on a major, because the college didn't offer very many choices. Since I didn't know what I wanted for a career, I chose Christian Education as my major. This would prepare me to work in a church as a Christian Education Director, where I would be in charge of the Sunday School and Youth Activities.

I decided to attend a Baptist Church in Hollywood, after visiting several churches in the area. The minister was a former chaplain in the military, but he'd been at this church for several years. I was somewhat critical of him, because I felt he was not sufficiently gospel oriented. He was patient with my overzealousness, however.

Mom and Carl worked at the run-down hotel in Hollywood only a couple months. Drug addicts lived there, so we weren't anxious to be there very long. Their next job was at a very modern hotel, also in Hollywood. Finally, that spring we moved into an apartment in Beverly Hills, one that I'll always remember as one of my favorite homes. It had two bedrooms and one and a half baths. I got the master bedroom with my own private bathroom.

Although I lived in the college dorm during the week, I went home almost every weekend. I especially loved the weekends spent in this Beverly Hills apartment.

There was a large park down the street where, one Saturday, I met a fellow and we talked for a while. He was tall and good-looking, but I was hesitant to get involved. I didn't know whether he was a Christian, and unless I knew that he was, I didn't want to go further. He asked me what I was doing that evening. I told him that I was going to be busy, that I was going to watch the Billy Graham Crusade on television.

Another restriction Baptists had was that we didn't believe in going to the movies. This made it rather difficult for me that year, because I got the chance to go on two movie sets, *Gisha Boy* and *Big Country*. *Gisha Boy* was being filmed at Paramount Studios, and *Big Country* was filmed in the Mojave Desert. Even though I wasn't supposed to go to movies, I decided to watch the filmings. Although I was thrilled by seeing all of the stars, I couldn't help wondering if I should be there. Was this any different from being at a theater watching a movie? Was I any less guilty of sin? Regardless of right and wrong, I did enjoy the filmings.

Back at the college in L.A., I was becoming concerned about the division between what the Bible referred to as the "world," and our life space as believers, who were not of this world. The world I referred to consisted of unsaved people who drank, smoked, and went to movies. We did not. I would walk down the streets of downtown Los Angeles and think, these other people I see are of the world and are not part of our fellowship as Christians, so we have to remain separate from them.

We had good times at Trinity, however, with several recreational activities which were organized by a team of our school's young college men and women. One morning, a fellow named Tom Peters stood on a table in the cafeteria and led his group of entertainers. I couldn't help but notice how good looking he was. He was tall, blond, had a good physique, and I also liked his voice. From then on, I noticed Tom around school.

Tom had been going with a girl who played the piano during Chapel. It was rumored that were breaking up. A party was coming up, one to which the girls invited the guys. I decided to ask Tom. It would be the perfect chance to get to know him. A couple of days later, I saw him after Chapel, and said, "Tom, would you like to go to the party with me?"

He looked surprised, but pleased, and replied, "Sure, Liz!"

During the next few days, Tom approached me several times, apparently in an attempt to get to know me better, but I reacted strangely around him. One night, he sat down with me at dinner. That didn't go too badly, but I wasn't quite sure how to act, so we just sat and ate quietly. The next day, as I was leaving the cafeteria after lunch, Tom came up beside me, evidently to walk around with me. But, I felt so strange. All my experiences from years of dating before were of no help. Tom started walking one direction. Instead of going with him, I walked in the other direction. I knew I'd acted oddly, but I didn't know how to act normally with Tom.

What might have begun as a close relationship between Tom and me fizzled out because of my ineptness. The trouble was, I was still crazy about him, but after my faux pas that day, Tom stopped pursuing me, to my dismay. We went to the party that weekend, but I didn't do any better. We were both so quiet that I left him after the party feeling I didn't know him any better than I had before. My problems with relating to Tom became more pronounced as the weeks went by. I would walk up to a small prayer room that overlooked the city, sit down and think, what can I do to get Tom interested in me? I'll die if this year ends and we're not dating. What if one of us doesn't return to school here next year, and I never see him again? That would be awful. I won't think about it.

That Spring I had started noticing symptoms that troubled me. I had tingling feelings in my arms and legs, similar to the way one's limbs feel when they're asleep. The feelings came and left without my arms or legs actually being asleep. This was unusual enough to alarm me. I also began to feel other abnormal sensations. As a child I'd asked my mother, "What does it mean to be nervous or anxious? I've never felt that way." But that spring at L.A. Trinity Bible College, I knew. The continual lack of sleep, constant working/studying, and the lack of exercising, since Trinity had no physical education classes that year, were all taking their toll. My sour love life with Tom was devastating, and didn't help any.

One of my friends at school, Carolyn Price, told me she thought she was having mental problems. She was concerned about her health and whether or not she would be able to continue school. As she told me this, I thought, maybe I'm headed for a nervous breakdown.

I looked for a solution to my emotional problems by trying to become a better Christian, by improving my spiritual life. I would go to a prayer closet in our dorm and try praying for longer periods of time. The problem with this was that I found it hard to concentrate. Instead, I ended up feeling more anxious.

Soon after that, our yearbooks were distributed. Tom wrote in mine, "Well, I'll always remember your kindness to a poor, lonely bachelor. We had fun, eh?"

Even though I hoped Tom's having written "poor, lonely bachelor" was an encouragement to me, I couldn't bring myself to pursue his friendship more actively, nor did I even know how to go about doing that.

Then I discovered I had bad breath. One weekend at home in Beverly Hills, Mom said to me, "You know, Liz, I've noticed lately that your breath has been somewhat offensive. Are you more nervous or troubled? Do you think you need to see a dentist?"

I thought, that's all I need. I've had hardly any dates this last year, even though I'm friends with several guys. It's probably all due to halitosis.

Earlier that spring I'd signed up to go on a missionary trip for the summer. Representatives from various groups had visited Trinity and taken names of interested students. I had signed up. Now that summer was near, and I was not feeling well, I took every chance that I could to get sleep and rest. I had only four days after classes ended before I was to leave on the trip to Mt. Rainier in Washington State, where I was assigned as a missionary. I couldn't seem to get the rest I needed, and I wondered if I should have made the commitment. Soon, five of us left on the trip north, all in the same car. When night came, I couldn't sleep in the car. I felt anxious and restless, but I didn't know what to do about those feelings, and no one was able to help me.

We arrived in a small town near Mt. Rainier, and went to the home of our supervisor for the summer, John Blakely. He and his wife began our training program. I felt terrible by then, but couldn't talk about it. The girl assigned as my partner, Gail Bridges, noticed my struggle. She later told me that she had wondered why she'd had the bad luck of being assigned to such a "blah" partner. I went through our training sessions feeling like an empty shell, and unable to pay attention.

Our summer missionary assignment was made up of three different locations. Gail's and my first assignment was at a small town near Mt. Rainier. We were hosted by a family who had a small cabin on their property. We slept in sleeping bags outside, and we were closer to Mt. Rainier than I'd ever been before. We were without a car and had little money, so we rode bicycles up and down the hills to get around.

I still couldn't sleep, and I had headaches most of the time. I wouldn't take aspirin, because I didn't want to rely on medicine. I would lie awake until 4:00 a.m., and then sleep until 6:00 a.m., when we had to get up.

I decided I was having a nervous breakdown. I wanted to confirm my diagnosis. I found out that our hostess had encyclopedias, so I looked up "nervous breakdown." I looked under "n," but there was no such listing. The book called my symptoms "neurasthenia." I read the definition, and it described the way I felt. I was right. I was having emotional problems.

After a few weeks at one location, we were sent on to another small town where we continued to set up summer Bible schools. We would also go to the family's homes, giving out tracts and witnessing to our faith.

Somehow, as the summer progressed, I became disillusioned with my religion and some of its restrictive aspects. I still believed in Christ. And I trusted in Him for my salvation. It was just that all-Bible, all-witnessing, no-worldliness, and constant-work-and-strain was too difficult for me. I wished I could go home to California and forget all of this for a while. I no longer felt positive about handing out tracts to strangers and asking them whether or not they had ever accepted Jesus Christ as their Lord and Savior. I felt too drained to do that. I wanted to sleep and relax and do all those good things I'd missed out on for so long.

I felt as though it had been forever since I'd relaxed. Every year I'd gone to school, danced, played the piano and the cello, then every summer I'd worked. The previous year I'd gone to college while working, and, finally, now I was a summer missionary. Would pushing myself never end? I was about to bring it to an end, at least for a while.

When I told John I planned to quit my missionary service before our third assignment, he wasn't pleased. He called me a "quitter," but I couldn't worry about that. John had to find Gail a new partner, and the third assignment was altered accordingly. I knew I had to rest and recover. Mother was due to fly to Seattle for my cousin Stephen's graduation from medical school. I planned to go back to California with Mom.

While I was in Washington, Mom and Carl were moving from Beverly Hills to Redondo Beach. Carl finally got a job back with the government, in the Redondo Beach Post Office. We temporally rented a house while looking for one to buy. After returning to California, I decided to rest, and not work. My schedule went haywire. I would sleep until 3:00 or 4:00 every afternoon. If I didn't sleep that much, I didn't feel right. I stayed up until 1:00 each morning. On the days I awoke earlier than 2:00 p.m., and couldn't go back to sleep, I felt miserable.

In the middle of the night I would often sit and think about my religious experience. I began reconsidering my concepts and attitudes about the world and those in it, both Christians and non-Christians. I decided I shouldn't limit my interactions to people based only on their beliefs. When I let go of these preconceived beliefs, I felt freer, more relaxed, and less guilty. Often my late-night thinking sessions were the best parts of my "days."

We continued our house-hunting project and finally decided upon a home in the Hollywood Riviera in Redondo Beach. It was the foothill to the Palos Verdes Hills. From our home, we could see the Pacific Ocean and the cities below. The best views were seen driving up and down the hill. Our house did not have the most fantastic view, which many of the other homes had, but we did have a view of the ocean.

I loved this home. It became the perfect environment for my project of rest, relaxation, and renewal. I would walk our Samoyed dog, Mitzie, down the hill to the beach and sit with her on the cliffs, watching the breakers roll in. Many times I felt peace fill my soul and mind, the healing of the rest and relaxation that I needed so much. Mitzie was a good companion.

When we moved to Redondo Beach, Mom took a job with a young general practitioner. She asked him for his advice about my emotional condition, and she arranged for me to talk to him. When I saw Dr. Williams, he didn't spend much time discussing my emotional problems. Rather, he discussed with me my plans for continuing college. His prescription for my condition was iron tablets, because I was anemic, and he also wanted me to get lots of exercise.

For exercise, I decided to take more dancing lessons. I also roller-skated twice a week at a rink. I no longer felt dancing was sinful, and I enjoyed roller skating. I didn't want to work fulltime, but I did want to earn money for clothes, so I took a job in a local dress shop three days a week. The dress shop was owned by a nice couple and their grown daughter.

On the days I was home, I did a lot of the cleaning that Mom had a hard time completing. I began to feel domestic and to think maybe it was about time for me to catch a husband. I was nineteen then. It looked like I wouldn't make it back to college, at least not anytime soon. This was the first time in my life that I'd considered planning for marriage. I'd always had so many things I wanted to do that I never had time to think about getting married.

I didn't want to return to L.A. Trinity. I applied to another Christian college near Los Angeles. I had a very good grade-point average, and was accepted. However, the school was more expensive, and I didn't want to work to pay for my tuition again. I'd gotten so exhausted from working and going to school the previous year that I couldn't bear to put myself through that again. So I didn't go to any college.

Another major project that fall was picking a church to join. I decided that a Baptist Church was no longer the answer, at least not for me at that time. So, Mom and I visited several churches and prayed for guidance in our decision. The day we visited St. Andrew's Presbyterian Church, we knew it was the right one for us. I was looking for a less fundamentalist church. It was in a Baptist Church that Christ had redeemed me, but I had let my Christian experience become so narrow-minded and unhealthy. Mom also felt this Presbyterian Church was the right one for her.

We enjoyed many Sunday mornings at St. Andrew's, especially Reverend Miller's sermons. In the college-age group I found rich fellowship and wholesome fun. The first Sunday night I went to this group, I walked into the church, wondering what I would find. Would the others like me? Would I like them? From the time I entered the designated room and sat down with the group, it felt right. That church, in conjunction with the local Methodist and Christian Churches, formed the college-age group. The three churches rotated as hosts, spending four months at each church. Although I came to the meeting with a question mark in my mind, I went home with an exclamation mark. I knew that I would enjoy this experience.

I also began lessons at a local dancing studio. Dr. Williams told me about the South Bay Light Opera Company, a group of actors, dancers, and singers, who put on plays in Redondo Beach. Although the members of the group were amateurs rather than professionals, most of them were ready to go professional. Dr. Williams told me that, in his opinion, the plays that this light opera company put on were every bit as well done as the professional plays in Hollywood.

I tried out for a dancing part in their newest production, "Girl Crazy." I was accepted, and soon afterward started rehearsals almost every weeknight. I was excited, and I got lots of exercise.

Once again my life was becoming healthier, more relaxed and enjoyable. On the mornings I was at home, I slept until 11:00 or 12:00. I'd fix myself a good breakfast of bacon, eggs, juice, and toast. The big breakfast seemed to satisfy more than my hunger, and it got my day off to a good start.

Dr. Williams had prescribed a mild medication, Deaner, one doctors usually prescribed for children rather than for adults. It was given to me to nourish and strengthen my brain and nervous system. This medicine was to be taken only when I felt it necessary. I abided by the doctor's orders and only took it a few times. Soon the exercise helped me feel a lot better, and I stopped taking Deaner.

After eating, I often took walks down the hill with Mitzie. I'd think, it's so nice not to rush to get somewhere by some specified time, but rather to just get close to nature and let its pace be my pace. I don't want to rush through life anymore; it's not worth it. This concept of avoiding too fast a pace was a large factor in my decisions that year. I said to Mom and Carl several times, "Don't expect me to rush around from place to place anymore. I've spent too much of my life rushing, and I'm not going to live my life that way any longer. You see all those cars on the freeway over there, racing from place to place? They're caught up in this mad race, too. What's the point of it all? There isn't any. When we come to the end of our lives and meet our Maker, will we receive any greater reward for having raced around? I doubt it."

By this time, I was getting to the place where too much discussion of Christian beliefs, at least those narrow-minded in nature, distressed me. I was sorting out my own feelings and, in doing so, realized that very strict concepts were not particularly healthy for me. When I would hear discussions similar to many I'd participated in myself earlier in my Christian experience, I felt uneasy, as though maybe I should feel guilty for leaving my former beliefs. But, at the same time, how could getting healthier mentally be wrong? One of my girlfriends from the Bible College lived in Palos Verdes Estates, nearby. We got together several times. When I told her of my new feelings toward my faith, she expressed concern. One day, she said to me, "You were such a great witness last year at school. So many people admired your strong faith. Don't do anything that will lessen your witness, please, Liz."

I realized her concern, but I also knew that I had to struggle with my own emotional condition and its cure. All the while, I felt the Lord was with me in my struggle regarding my Christian beliefs.

That fall, I still found myself thinking about Tom. The situation was somewhat similar to my former reminiscences about Bill when we first moved from Washington to California. I'd been told that Tom would be attending Bob Jones University in the southern part of the United States that fall. I decided I would write him, hoping he would receive my letter and write back. The only trouble with this scheme was that I didn't have his exact address, just the name of the school and the city and state in which it was located. I thought that if the letter didn't reach him, it would be returned to me. I wrote to Tom, but never heard from him, nor did I get the letter back. This left me frustrated. I didn't know whether he'd received it. I decided I'd done all I could, and now I had to let the matter rest. I probably would never see him or hear from him again.

Meanwhile, I was dating again and happy with that state of affairs. I went out with several young men from church, and also met quite a few eligible men at the local skating rink. One fellow, in particular, I dated, Jerry, was Italian. He'd been married and divorced and was helping support his ex-wife and their small daughter. As he began to show more interest in me and a desire for a closer relationship, my reaction was to hold back because he was divorced. I hoped someone else might come along sometime soon.

Chapter Seven

A MARRIAGE?

St. Louis, 1960

During the Christmas season that year, as I was thinking about friends and relatives to whom I wanted to send cards and letters, I thought about Mario. I believed he probably still lived in St. Louis, so I found his address and sent him a card with a note. I thought it would be nice to hear from him and catch up on what had happened in his life since the couple of letters we exchanged after his return to St. Louis two years before.

To my surprise, shortly afterwards I received a letter from Mario, but not from St. Louis. It was from New Mexico. Once again, he was temporarily based out-of-state, working in the space program. I wrote and told him I'd like to see him again if he ever got a chance to drive from New Mexico to California. He replied, saying he'd be in California to see me over the coming Easter holiday.

Jerry had discussed marrying me, and he was unhappy to hear about Mario's visit. I had to search my heart to decide which one I wanted to encourage and which one to discourage. It wasn't easy. Mario had planned to arrive on the last night of our performance of *Girl Crazy*. I hoped he would be able to see the show, as I had expressed to him in my previous letter. I was still dating Jerry, but I was excitedly awaiting Mario's visit.

Mario arrived around 10:00 a.m., the day after our performance. This was disappointing, but I was still glad to see him. I hadn't been up very long when the doorbell rang. I thought, it's a good thing I didn't sleep any later. Here he is. Happily, I quickly walked to the door, rubbing away the sleep remaining in my eyes.

"Liz, you're every bit as beautiful as you were two years ago," Mario said, as we took our first look at each other.

"I'm glad you weren't here any earlier," I replied. "I haven't been up very long." I hoped he wouldn't think I was lazy.

Mario smiled and said, "Let's go for a ride. It's such a nice day. I'd like to see your Pacific Ocean again."

"Okay, Mario, we can stop by the dress shop where I work. I'd like you to meet the owners, Mr. and Mrs. Carter, and their daughter, Alexis." Later at the store, everyone was delighted to meet Mario, and said he was an extremely handsome man. All my friends and relatives were excited, speaking highly of Mario, and giving us their approval.

On the first day Mario and I were together, during our ride to the ocean, he asked me to marry him once again; I was thrilled, but concerned. He must really love me, I thought. He's so eager to get married, but I hope he won't rush me into a hasty decision. Marriage is such an important undertaking. During Mario's visit, we went to parties, to Disney Land, we even danced to Lawrence Welk. I had a great week.

I didn't know what decision to make, whether to tell Mario "yes" or "no." He certainly was good looking. No one could deny that fact. Also, from what he told me, he made excellent money on his job. I wasn't sure how I'd feel about being the wife of someone "well-to-do." I'd always felt I would not want to be rich. That did not seem appealing to me. I also wasn't sure whether or not I was in love with him. Evidently he is crazy about me, I concluded. The more I thought about our relationship, the more I believed I could grow to love him.

There were several times that week, when riding with Mario in his car, that I'd look at him and experience a strange feeling, a sort of a foreboding sensation. I wondered if it could be apprehension about my pending decision. I looked at him and I saw his outward handsomeness, but I sensed something; I was not sure just what it was.

Since my faith in Christ was still strong, I decided to pray about the decision I was to make. I knelt by my bed that evening and prayed, "Dear Lord, help me know if I should marry Mario. Help me know Your will in this decision. I know that he's a man I've been involved with before. Maybe for that reason, I should marry him. Or, maybe there will be someone else You intend for me. Please help me know what to do."

Mario asked me several times that week about my decision. I finally told him to let me have a couple of weeks to decide. I asked him to write me when he got back to St. Louis, and I'd write him back my answer.

He agreed. He was only able to be in California for one week, which didn't give me enough time to make such an important decision.

Mario left, and I continued to mull over his proposal. I got an idea for solving my dilemma. I would go to St. Louis, get a job, and a place to live. That way I could see more of Mario in his own environment. Then I'd be able to make a better decision.

I mentioned this plan to Mom, but she said, "No, I don't think you should do that. You're too young to go to a new city and live alone." So that squelched my plan. I was left with a major decision to make with very few facts to go on.

As I continued praying, it seemed as though the right answer was that I should marry Mario. This way, the man I married would be the second one I'd had a sexual relationship with, but if I married another man, he would then be my third. I couldn't marry my first, Bill, because he was already married. I remembered from studying the Old Testament, that there was a law stating that if a young man and woman had sexual intercourse, they had to marry or face the penalty of death. I knew no one would kill me if I married another man, but I wanted to abide by God's law.

I finally wrote Mario that I would marry him. He was sending me many love letters full of his thoughts about us. Mario wrote, asking what kind of engagement ring I'd like. I wrote back that I wanted a white gold ring with a single diamond. He wrote me back and said that would be what he would buy me. Shortly afterward, I received my ring. It had a rather large center diamond with several smaller diamonds on the sides. I was pleased because it was a beautiful ring; however, it was not exactly what I had asked for.

A couple of weeks later, I discovered the large diamond was coming loose. I took it to a jeweler for tightening. When I told him my ring was new, he replied, "I don't believe this is a new ring. If it were, the setting would not be loose."

I couldn't help thinking about what the jeweler said. Mario had indicated he was buying me a ring. Was it a used ring? If not, why did the setting loosen? And, why had Mario asked me to pick a style and then send me something different? Oh well, I thought, I won't worry about it.

We decided to have our wedding in St. Louis that August. I wanted it to be in California, but Mario wanted to have our wedding in his home city, so I agreed. Mom and I would fly to St. Louis in July to prepare for the ceremony.

With the money I'd earned that spring, I bought my trousseau. I received a discount at the dress shop and was able to buy several articles of clothing. A good friend of our family, who lived nearby, threw a shower for me, and I received beautiful lingerie from my girlfriends.

One thing that Mario didn't seem to like was my new religiousness. He said to me one day that spring, "Liz, you sure have become more religious since the first time we dated. Why do you write Bible verse references at the end of all your letters to me? I've never seen anyone do that before. It is unusual."

"Well, Mario, I'm not sure how common it is, but in answer to your question, yes, I have become more religious. Since we last went together, I've become a born-again Christian. That's why I write Bible references. I want to share my new faith."

Mario's expression definitely indicated that he didn't understand my change of beliefs. Even knowing that I'd changed so much, he still was ardent in his letters to me and never suggested that he wanted to call off our wedding.

Early that summer, I went up to Seattle to be in my friend Jean Johnson's wedding. I caught the bridal bouquet, which seemed perfect since my wedding was only two months away. Grandma Jones also had a shower for me, inviting several friends from Kenniltown and Seattle. At this shower, I received many lovely household gifts. While in Seattle, I received a letter from Mario that shocked me. He had indicated that he made quite a good salary. In the letter I received, Mario confessed that he had exaggerated about his salary. He then told me his true salary, which was considerably less. I didn't quite know what to think. Jean and I discussed the situation, but my decision still remained to marry Mario. Since I'd been worried that he was too rich for me, how could I now worry if he wasn't rich after all? I was, however, disappointed that he'd lied to me. Some of Mario's charisma was fading.

Mario also wrote me that his son was not as young as he'd previously told me. He wrote that Tommy was thirteen years old. Before, he'd also mentioned that his first wife died giving birth to their son, Tommy. Now he admitted that she had not died giving birth to their son, but they'd been divorced when Tommy

117

was a baby. Mario's wife asked him to raise the boy after the divorce. To now find out that Tommy wasn't four, but thirteen, only six years younger than I, was exasperating. How would I feel having such a mature stepson? All of this came as a shock to me, but even that was not as surprising as Mario's next revelation that he was actually thirty-eight years old. This meant that he was not ten years older then I, as he previously stated, but nineteen years older. I wondered if Mario's deceptions about his life had represented the basis for the foreboding sensation I felt while previously making my decision whether or not to marry him. Still my decision remained solid. I had committed myself; I would follow through.

We, Mom, Mario, and I, had lots to do in St. Louis, and the wedding turned out to be beautiful. We were married in the chapel of a brick colonial Presbyterian Church. There were about sixty guests, just the right number to fill the chapel. Mom's brother Uncle Gerald and Aunt Phyllis came down from Iowa for the wedding. Aunt Phyllis was my Matron of Honor.

We spent our honeymoon in the beautiful Ozarks. It wasn't easy for Mario to afford the honeymoon, but I wanted one so badly. I wouldn't have it any other way. Mario didn't argue the matter. I believed that every bride and groom had to have their honeymoon. To me, there was no other option. It wasn't the greatest honeymoon, however. The things we did such as horseback riding, swimming, and so on, were fine, and the country was beautiful. The problem was my relationship with Mario. Mario expressed to me that he felt my mother was overbearing. One evening at dinner he made some comments about Mom that I didn't like. This put a damper on my mood for the rest of our honeymoon. I thought, how can he love me if he dislikes my mother? I've never heard anyone say such unfavorable things about her.

I felt somewhat zombie-like for the rest of the trip. I knew these should be the most wonderful days of our lives, but it seemed a big disappointment. Somehow, Mario didn't talk the same way to me as he had before. There was not as much affection or attention in his behavior. I felt as though there were barriers building between us.

I had been fitted with a diaphragm before the wedding. I had it with me but I didn't like the way it felt, so I didn't use it much. I told myself, I'm married now, so if I get pregnant it won't matter.

The evening we arrived back in St. Louis from the Ozarks, we went over to see some of Mario's friends. I'd gotten to know them before the wedding, but I felt strange being around them. They were all middle-aged and enjoyed sitting around talking and drinking coffee. I wanted to skate, bowl, or dance instead. Mario's friends had been really nice to me, even though I found them to be unexciting.

That night, after returning from our honeymoon, something strange happened. We were at Mario's sister Marie's house. We were sitting around talking when Mario said, "Why don't we play a game?"

I responded with enthusiasm, "Sure, what game do you want to play?"

"It goes like this," Mario continued. "Someone's wife goes upstairs to the bedroom, gets undressed and into bed. Then someone else's husband goes upstairs …"

"You mean," I interrupted, "that woman's husband!"

"No," Mario replied, "I mean someone else's husband. He goes up there, gets undressed, and gets into bed with the woman. The point is to see if nothing happens."

I had been leaning back in my chair listening to Mario, but after processing what he had just said, I jerked forward, landing the chair on all four legs, and exclaimed, "Well, if that's the kind of games you people play, you can count me out!" I definitely didn't want to participate in their activities, whatever they represented, and I wanted everyone there to know that.

The next morning, Mario said to me, while we were still in bed, "Why couldn't you have gotten along better last night at Marie's? I'm really disappointed in you."

I knew I wanted no part of Mario's games. I didn't tell him that I would change my mind and participate in his disgusting activities. Perhaps that was what he hoped for. I simply responded to his question, "I don't know why you feel that my not playing your repulsive game is so terrible. It sounded pretty indecent to me!"

I told Mario I hadn't had sex with anyone after our sexual relationship two years before. He replied, "Oh, Liz, I don't believe that!" However, it was true. From then on, Mario's and my relationship continued to worsen. He never hugged or kissed me, nor did he say anything that indicated he still loved me. I grew discouraged and disappointed.

Another evening, when he came home from work, I said to him, "You know when you think about it, marriage sure lasts a long time. We're going to be together for so many years. It's hard to comprehend."

Mario didn't say much at first, but we later discussed at great length the problem of whether or not we should continue our marriage. Mario mentioned several times that whenever he brought up the topic of my returning to California, I seemed happier. I was unhappy with our relationship and all that was lacking in it since our wedding, both physically and emotionally. It was hard for me to adjust to the transition from Mario's continuous love and affection to his new coldness. Maybe this is a common situation with newlyweds, I thought, but that didn't lessen my despair. I believed it was more likely a reflection of our poor relationship, which had been built upon very little.

Then, one Sunday afternoon, when Mario and I had dinner with his mother, she shocked me when she said, "Liz, you are Mario's fourth wife." That was certainly news to me, but the next morning Mario denied what she said. Being his fourth wife certainly was much different from the lie that Mario told me about only being divorced once. Now I learned that I was his fourth wife, and I could see the trail of Mario's lies that started to cloud our relationship.

To add to these problems, I was feeling sick in the mornings. I was used to sleeping until at least 7:00 a.m., but now I had to get up at 5:30 a.m. to get Mario off to work. Then I'd go back to bed. Soon afterwards, I'd get up again to get Tommy ready for to school. I went back to bed after Tommy left, and tried to sleep until 9:00 a.m. Even going back to sleep, when I awoke I didn't feel rested. I couldn't figure out why I was so drained of energy in the mornings. This made it hard to take care of my duties as a wife and mother. Later in the day, I would start feeling better and get a lot of housework done. However, between all my chores and lack of transportation, I felt trapped in our trailer.

I asked Mario shortly after we were married if I could learn how to drive and get a car, so I could get around. We were living in a trailer out in what was called, "The County." The only place I was able to go during the days while Mario was at work was to the laundromat once a week with a neighbor. I got bored in the trailer all day, cleaning and cooking. There were no buses that ran near our trailer park; a car seemed to be the answer. Mario responded that he wouldn't buy me a car, at least not right then.

Our discussions continued about whether we should stay together. Mom had written me several times and I hadn't answered. When I finally wrote her, I explained our dilemma. She was furious and sent her reply right away. She wrote that Mario should be mature enough to help me get accustomed to married life, and that, rather than encouraging a divorce, he should be doing everything in his power to keep the marriage intact. Mom also wrote that she was amazed we'd even discussed a divorce, especially so soon. In the letter, she wrote, "People don't get married to begin figuring out how to break up!"

When I would think about breaking up with Mario, I visualized myself going to work as a sophisticated career woman. No longer would I be made to do monotonous housework day in and day out. I also mentioned to Mario several times that if we did split up, maybe we could get back together later after I'd finished college and had my career. He told me that sounded like a pipe dream.

I'm sure I contributed some to the change in Mario's behavior. I often criticized him for several things he did that I didn't like. I got after him for swearing, smoking, his table manners, to name a few bad habits. He didn't appreciate my nagging, and it didn't help our marriage. Mario's attitude regarding money did not help matters either.

Mario was interested in my family's financial situation. One day he said to me, "Liz, I thought your Uncle Gerald in Iowa would send us a check for a few thousand dollars as a wedding present. Why didn't he?"

"I don't know whatever gave you the idea he would do that," I replied. "He and Aunt Phyllis bought my veil and Mom's dress. We couldn't have expected more than that."

"And, I thought your other uncle in Miami, the yacht broker, would give us a boat." Mario seemed to think we were going to receive all sorts of elaborate presents from my family.

He continued, "What about all your wealthy family on your father's side? Why didn't we hear from them?"

"Mario," I countered, "I've never even met my real father. My grandfather died six years ago. We're not in touch with our other relatives on Father's side. Yes, they do have money, but that doesn't affect us."

Mario expressed the way he felt about our possessions when he told me, "What's mine is mine, and what's yours is mine" That didn't make me feel any better. When I heard him make that statement, I thought, I guess Mario just wants control over all money and possessions. Was I only another possession to him? Had he married me for my money?

Mario wanted to quit working at the aircraft company where he'd worked for many years, and open his own Italian restaurant. One Saturday, he took a friend and me to look at some prospective locations. One place in particular was very nice. The problem with it was that he needed around $40,000 to get it going, and he had nowhere near that amount of funds. He asked if my parents could give him $10,000.00? I told him they wouldn't be able to do that. To me this reaffirmed that he was looking for money from my family, and I didn't like that at all.

We didn't tell Mario's mother or our friends in St. Louis about the possibility of ending our marriage. How could we announce the failure of our marriage so soon? We had only been married for two months.

It was the middle of October. I was a few weeks overdue for my period and I had always been very regular. I had my last period just before the wedding. I decided I'd better go see a gynecologist and find out if I might be pregnant. About a week later, I finally visited a gynecologist. After examining me, she told me that it was too soon for her to tell whether or not I was going to have a baby, and that I should come back in two weeks if I didn't get my period.

Mario waited for me in his car. On our drive home, I explained to him what the doctor had said. Then I said, "Maybe we should wait until I see the doctor in two weeks before I leave for California. I might be pregnant. If I am, maybe we should stay together."

"You can find that out when you get back to California," he replied. "I've already paid for the plane ticket. We won't change plans."

I was crushed. Even though Mario and I might be having a baby, he didn't want to try to make our marriage work. Oh well, I thought, maybe I will be happier at home. I guess I don't have any other choice. As the distance between us grew, Mario seemed to care less about my feelings. One night he brought me into our bedroom, which was welcomed attention after the long period without any physical contact. He seemed ready to make love to me as we had done before. Then once we entered the bedroom, he pushed me on the bed and onto my stomach. Trusting him, I lay down, not expecting what he was going to do next. He then placed his penis into my anus, and had intercourse with me there. This was confusing and frightening, and something I had never experienced before or even heard about. All I wanted to do was get away from him. I vowed I would never let any man take advantage of me that way again. Mario had lost his charisma and my trust; I no longer felt this relationship would work.

About two months after our wedding, Mario and I separated. I'll never forget the last night before I flew home. We stood close to each other, looking in our large bedroom mirror. I turned to him and said, "We sure do make a good looking couple, don't we? I bet our baby will be beautiful."

Mario agreed.

Then, when we went to bed, Mario reached over, put his arm around my waist, and said, "Maybe we shouldn't split up after all."

"Mario," I replied, "Everything is set to go. I'll go home." This was the first time he'd expressed to me that he might have a change of heart about our pending separation. I became confused. Hadn't Mario been the one who had pushed me to go home, even when he found out I might be pregnant? Why was he bringing this up now?

In the middle of one October night, Mario drove me to what I believed was the airport. He had said that I was flying first class. I was surprised to discover that the plane wasn't a commercial airline at all, but some sort of military plane. It was small, and there were no regular passengers, just staff from either the aircraft company where he worked or the military. I thought, typical of Mario, another lie.

There was a storm that night. I heard some of the men say they were afraid we wouldn't make it to California. That wasn't very comforting. But we did get there. I got off the plane and met Mom and Carl. They had left me in St. Louis a newlywed, but I returned to them in California a broken woman separated from her husband. I had never felt so low. With the failure of my marriage, I thought, maybe Carl was right all along. I would never succeed at being a wife.

Dr. Williams had me go for a frog test to determine if I was pregnant. Sure enough, the results were positive. Even though my marriage was ending, I wasn't unhappy about the test results. I'd always said I wanted to have children while I was young.

Mario soon surprised me with another problem. When I told him over the phone that I was pregnant, his response was, "How do I know I'm the father? Someone else could have gotten you pregnant, for all I know!"

"Mario, you may think a crazy thought like that," I told him, "but I know who the father is. It could be no one but you, believe me!" I decided that Mario must be full of surprises. I knew Mario was the father of my child, regardless of what he thought or made up.

About this time, Aunt Phyllis and Uncle Gerald called me. They were concerned about Mario's and my situation, and offered to let me come back to Iowa and stay with them to see if Mario and I could work things out.

"But, Uncle Gerald, it won't work," I told him. "You don't know all the experiences I've just been through."

I told him about the various happenings in St. Louis and the reasons why I felt reconciliation was impossible. It was quite a traumatic conversation for me. I felt threatened at even the suggestion of returning to St. Louis and Mario. After I finished explaining, Uncle Gerald agreed that Mario's and my marriage had not worked out, that perhaps we could not be reconciled.

My thoughts were changing regarding other people who were getting a divorce or had been divorced. I had been so judgmental before my own separation. I thought back to the day before my marriage when a woman had come into the dress shop in Redondo Beach. She was telling us that her husband was in the process of disowning her bills, and that they were divorcing. When I heard her conversation, I said, "I'm getting married myself, but I don't believe in divorce. I'll never get a divorce because, as far as I'm concerned, it's wrong."

"That's just how I always felt before this happened to me," she had replied.

At the time, I just looked at her, thinking to myself, you're doing something wrong. Divorce is a sin.

Now that I was back in California and headed for a divorce myself, my attitude was different. It was a humbling experience. Now the great Christian woman who could do no wrong was just as much a sinner as anyone. I was not holier than others, after all, or holier than the woman in the dress shop; nor was I holier than Jerry or his ex-wife.

One night, at the church group, I saw Jerry and expressed my realization to him. He listened, but seemed more interested in other matters. Before long, he left me and returned to the other young people. He had a new girlfriend, and he no longer needed or wanted me.

Mario wasn't sending me any money. Carl insisted I must get a job if I wanted to stay with him and Mom. Mom went along with him in order to have peace, but I contended, "How can I get a job if I'm pregnant?"

Mom suggested I not tell potential employers I was pregnant. Although deception went against my principles, I finally agreed to their plan. I was a good typist. I'd taken typing two years in high school. I hadn't taken shorthand, however, so I set out to find a clerk-typist job. I found one, but the problem was that I had to have a physical. I knew that would never work out, because I would have to admit my condition.

"What was the date of your last period?" The doctor stood in front of me as I sat on his examination table.

"Sometime toward the middle of August."

132

"Have you considered the possibility that you may be pregnant?"

"I know I'm pregnant," I answered. "I need a job, so I didn't tell Mr. O'Neil at the office about it. I see now that I was wrong to try and hide my pregnancy. I won't take up any more of your time."

I rejoined Mom in the waiting room, and told her what had happened. A few minutes later, the doctor came out of his office. He asked me, "Are you sure you want to remain pregnant?" This question shocked me almost as much as Mario's proposal for his "game" in St. Louis.

"Of course I want to remain pregnant! I wouldn't have it any other way."

After all, I reminded myself, wasn't I the one who said to Mario a couple of days after our return from the Ozarks, "Wouldn't it be nice to have a baby around to take care of?"

Mario replied that he wanted to wait a couple of years before we had any children. He wanted to make sure our marriage was going to work. Little did I know that I was already pregnant at that time. After leaving the doctor's office, I told Mr. O'Neil what had happened. I decided to only apply for jobs with temporary openings for the coming Christmas Season, so that I would not be working further into my pregnancy.

There was a new shopping center in town just down the hill from us. I got a sales job for the holidays at a clothing store. There was no need to tell my employer about being pregnant, because by the time I would begin to "show," the job would be over.

As Christmas approached, I received a letter from Mario. He was going to drive to California to see me for a couple of days over the holidays. I was shocked, but I was definite in my decision not to reconcile with him. I dreaded his arrival.

The night he arrived however, I was distressed and confused. When I opened the door, there he stood as handsome as ever, the father of my unborn child. I felt love for him, but I simultaneously felt fear. How could I love and fear the same man, I wondered? Because I found myself feeling positive feelings for him, I asked Mom whether she minded if Mario stayed with us. Evidently, she wasn't experiencing the same emotions as I. Carl had been insistent that Mario not be allowed in our house at all. Mom suggested that he find a motel room nearby. Mario and I spent time together for the next couple of days, and we had sex in his motel room. I justified those sexual relations in my mind because of the fact that we were still married.

I remember Mario driving us somewhere nearby in Palos Verdes, getting out of the car and walking with me close to a stream. He put his arms around my waist and said, "Liz, come back to St. Louis with me. You know, God means for couples to be together."

"I'm too confused, Mario," I answered. "You've only made me more confused by coming out here and saying these things. Please take me home."

Mario seemed to understand my confusion, and was sympathetic the next morning. He drove me to work and asked me, once more, if I would go back with him. I answered that I had to get to work, and my decision was still the same. Later he told me that he was upset when he saw me take off for work, leaving him in his car to drive back to St. Louis alone. He said I really seemed the sophisticated woman, so independent.

All I knew was how confused I was. Mario had insisted on marrying me. After the wedding he'd felt that maybe for my happiness we should divorce. Now he wanted to go back together. What did he really want? Besides that, what did I really want? Also, I had a child within me to consider. Mario brought

Christmas presents with him from St. Louis. As confused as I was, I appreciated his thoughtfulness.

Not long after he left, I came down with a virus and stayed home from work for a while. While sick in bed, I read *Gone With The Wind*. I'd never read the book, and found southern culture fascinating.

Finally, I called my boss and told him that I was sorry to miss work for so long. Then I revealed to him that I was pregnant. He was very nice and told me to come back to work when I was completely well, that everything at the store was fine, and for me not to worry.

Mom was, at this time, going through her own private hell, because Carl had not welcomed my return. He told Mom and me that, although he would allow me to stay with them, I would have absolutely no say in anything about their home, family concerns, or decisions. He said he had known all along Mario was "no good," even though he had approved our marriage.

Mom had to come to grips with her own life. Over the years, she had asked me several times if she should divorce Carl. Each time I told her that I wanted her to stay married, and that's what she did. She told me she couldn't understand how I could continue being nice to him, even though he was so nasty to me. However, now she was reconsidering her decision to stay with Carl. Would he make a good step-grandparent to her daughter's soon-to-be-born child? Or would he mistreat that new life the way he had already mistreated her only child? Maybe this would be as good a time as any to leave Carl. Maybe it would be her last chance to try to save the psychological health of her offspring.

Mom talked to her brother Gerald in Iowa about her problems. He suggested that she have her furniture moved out of their house without Carl being aware of it. Then she could secretly take off for Iowa and go to work for Uncle Gerald there. This sounded like a good solution to our problems with Carl. This would be a bold move, but she was running out of options.

Chapter Eight

MY FUTURE
MEETS MY PAST

Miami, 1961

A few days later, I had a pleasant surprise. I received a letter from Mom's brother Joseph in Miami. Hearing about my pregnancy and separation, he wrote to me, asking if I'd like to fly to Miami to visit him and his family. I was delighted to take him up on his offer. What a way to spend my pregnancy, vacationing in Florida. I had read about the islands of the Bahamas in *Gone With The Wind,* just a couple weeks before. At the time, I wondered if I'd ever get out to that part of the country. I'd never before been to the east coast and thought this would be a great opportunity. I accepted Uncle Joseph's invitation, informing him by return mail.

Things were beginning to look up. I was anxious to meet Uncle Joseph. I hadn't seen him since I was six months old, which was far too young for me to remember. I was also looking forward to meeting his wife, Aunt Beth, and his two little daughters, Barbara and Nancy.

A few days later, I shopped for maternity outfits suitable for Miami's winter weather. I had lots of fun buying my new wardrobe with money I earned that Christmas. I bought a black skirt with a matching black-and-white jumper top and a coordinating white blouse with a "Peter Pan" collar. I also bought a beautiful pair of blue plaid pants with a blue top. I had begun to show. As I tried on each article of clothing and viewed myself in the mirror, I could envision my stomach getting bigger as my baby showed itself to the world.

I'd never flown before, and I was eagerly anticipating my trip in an Electra Jet. I thought Uncle Joseph was the greatest uncle to send me a first-class ticket on the new Electra Jet all the way from Los Angeles to Miami.

Finally, the day arrived, and I was off to the east coast. For a while, I enjoyed looking at the ever-shifting and beautiful landscape of the earth below. Before long, however, I started talking to the attractive, middle-aged man seated next to me. I told him I was on my way to Miami to visit my uncle and his family. He told me that was his destination, as well. He said he lived in Miami but, in his line of work, he traveled quite a bit.

He asked my uncle's name. I told him, "Joseph Duncan." His immediate response was, "Not the Joseph Duncan that's so prominent in the Marine Counsel of the Miami Chamber of Commerce?"

"I don't know if he's active in that," I replied. "But that's his name. He probably is the man you're thinking of, however, because he is a yacht broker."

"Joe Duncan is very well known in Miami," he continued. "I don't know if he would even know who I am, but I've been involved in Chamber of Commerce activities that he has been very influential in organizing. Your uncle is very well known in Miami."

I was impressed. This dignified, executive-type man was impressed at the mention of Uncle Joseph's name. My trip was off to a good start, and this only made me more excited to meet Uncle Joseph.

Meanwhile, Mom was trying to end her thirteen-year relationship with Carl. The plan had now changed to her heading for Memphis from California, where she would leave her car, then fly to Miami and join me in visiting with Uncle Joseph and his family. Then, before I'd have my baby, we'd drive to Iowa, where, my mother's other brother, Uncle Gerald Duncan, was a practicing physician. I planned to have him deliver my child. We would find a place to live there in Des Moines, Iowa, and settle down.

Mom had discussed her marital problems with her boss, Dr. Williams. He had seen Carl once or twice as a patient. He told her that he could easily understand the problems we were having with Carl. She had asked him if he would prescribe Carl something to help calm him down. Carl had a habit of storming through the house, talking about killing this person or that person. Mom would often sleep in the other bed in my room and prop a chair up against the door, in case he would become violent and come after one of us. But Dr. Williams was afraid to give Carl anything, for fear of his retaliation if he were to find out what he'd been given.

Dr. Williams agreed with the suggestion Uncle Gerald had given Mom. He said she should have her furniture taken out of the house without Carl's knowledge and get herself safely away while he was at work. That way perhaps she could avoid any violent or drastic reaction he might have about her leaving him. He had threatened her before.

It seemed as though my martial crisis had become the climactic event which triggered Mom's decision that she herself could no longer remain in her marriage. She had tried hard to do the right thing, to maintain an intact family. But, she finally realized that no marriage would be better than a marriage to a dangerous, mentally ill partner. She regretted having married him at all, having so hastily wed a man partly because he kept after her for a decision, and also because her daughter had pushed for "a new daddy."

It would be hard for her to start a new life, to be single again after thirteen years of being a wife, but she decided she better muster the courage to deal with this problem and leave Carl. With God's help, there would be no harm to her or to those she loved.

****

Uncle Joseph was there to greet me at the Miami International Airport. Tagging along with him were his two adorable daughters. Little Nancy, just three years old, had blond, curly hair, so much like my hair at that age. And Barbara was a beautiful child, a little older, with long straight, darker blond hair.

"I'm sorry, Elizabeth," Uncle Joseph began as we walked to his car, "but Beth and I have to go out tonight. It's a shame that the affair we're going to is being held on the night you arrived, but I'm afraid it's important that we go. Beth's made some dinner for you and the girls, and we've arranged for a baby sitter, so hopefully you'll have a pleasant evening."

"Oh, that's fine, Uncle Joseph, but please call me Liz," I replied. After Uncle Joseph and Aunt Beth left for the evening, we all sat down and ate our delicious chicken dinner. Afterwards the girls went to bed, and I did the dishes. I went to bed around ten but woke up when I heard Aunt Beth and Uncle Joseph return. I'd been impressed with Aunt Beth's warmth and friendliness when we'd met earlier that evening. Now, hearing their soft voices in the Florida room, as family rooms are called in Miami, I found myself getting out of bed and going out to join them.

"Did we wake you, Liz?" asked Uncle Joseph.

"Oh, that's all right," I answered. "I was restless, anyway, and wasn't sleeping too well. Did you have a good time tonight?"

"Yes we did," replied Aunt Beth. "Tonight's affair had to do with the opening of Miami's new port, Dodge Island. Your Uncle Joseph was quite instrumental in developing this new port. It will make it possible to dock several ocean liners and other large ships in Miami."

"You, know," I commented, "now that you mention it, I sat next to a man on the plane who said he's worked with Uncle Joseph in the Miami Chamber of Commerce Marine Counsel. It's all very exciting!"

Aunt Beth and Uncle Joseph were warm people. I could feel the healing power of their love and the love in their family. A few days after I arrived in Miami, Aunt Beth had to go to the dentist's to have extensive dental work. She wasn't able to do her normal chores, so I tried to help some.

"Housecleaning, Liz?" It was Uncle Joseph. He'd just arrived home for lunch and found me sweeping their Florida room floor while Aunt Beth was recovering in the bedroom.

"Yes, I thought I would help with the cleaning some, since Aunt Beth's resting."

"You've been a big help while Beth's been recuperating," Uncle Joseph told me. "We all appreciate it."

Soon Aunt Beth was back to normal and I had a chance to get to know her better. Mornings we'd sit at their long dining room table and have a large breakfast. Aunt Beth introduced me to my first cup of coffee, which started my habit of drinking coffee in the mornings.

I found Aunt Beth's conversations fascinating. She told me about many different and interesting people. Once she told me how a famous Broadway producer had slept in the same guest room I was sleeping in. It was great, lounging around in the mornings this way; I found it refreshing and a good change of pace. Each morning after our coffee, Aunt Beth would say to me, "What would you like to do today, Sweetie?"

I thought this was great. Mom had been home very little while I was growing up. She'd always worked since we'd left Chicago. It was nice to be able to choose what to do each day with such a pleasant person as Aunt Beth.

At Aunt Beth and Uncle Joseph's we celebrated every holiday, Valentine's Day, birthdays, and Easter. Our parties seemed like "warm fuzzies" to me. In fact, I found the environment in this home very healing. I'd go to bed at night early, always with pleasant feelings. I knew my aunt and uncle cared for me, for each other, for their children, as well as for many others. Aunt Beth and Uncle Joseph provided a radiating love toward all who came into their lives. The environment was so much more healthy and positive than the home in which I'd grown up during the previous thirteen years.

Soon we received letters from Mom telling us she was on her way to Miami, and looking forward to seeing everyone. Uncle Joseph asked me often what the latest news was from Mom. He and Aunt Beth were anticipating her arrival, as well. Mom wrote that she had gone ahead and left their house while Carl was at work, having most of our furniture moved out and put into storage.

On Sundays, Uncle Joseph's family and I went to church, after eating a breakfast of pancakes prepared by Uncle Joseph. They also attended a Congregational Church. I still considered Congregational Churches too liberal for me, but I did truly enjoy the services. The minister had served at the church for many years, and he was a warm, dynamic person. The services were crowded to hear his sermons.

Billy Graham had a crusade in Miami while I was there. A neighbor took me with her to one of the services. I had mixed feelings; going to the service thrilled me, but I came away somewhat disturbed. I found myself experiencing the same, old constricted feelings I retained from my experiences in fundamentalist Christian churches. I realized how nice the neighbor was for taking me to see Billy Graham, but I decided not to attend any more services.

Soon Mom reached Miami, flying in from Memphis. We were happy to have her with us. One of her first concerns was that I meet Aunt Louise, Uncle Joseph's first wife. They had been married before for a long time, but they never had children. Later, they were divorced, and then Uncle Joseph married Aunt Beth. Mom also was impressed with how much I liked Aunt Beth.

Mother took me to meet Aunt Louise and her husband, whom she had married after being divorced from Uncle Joseph. Louise's stepson was an attorney in Miami. Since she had always been a legal secretary, Louise helped him set up a new practice as the head lawyer in his own firm. She was the office manager, did an excellent job, and was one of the reasons for his success.

I also loved Aunt Louise from the start. I was very impressed that Uncle Joseph did so well in two different marriages. I was somewhat upset about the situation of simultaneously meeting and loving both Aunt Beth and Aunt Louise. It was something I had to struggle with, adjust to, and live with. But right away, they were both so easy for me to love.

Shortly after arriving in Miami, I remembered that my father lived there. I knew his name, of course, and that he was an attorney, so I looked him up in the phone book. Sure enough, there he was. I told Aunt Beth and Uncle Joseph how much I'd like to meet him, but that Mom had been against my meeting him. She always told me how a good friend of the Scott family in Chicago had warned her not to let me know my father, that he would "ruin me." She told Mom that my father had visited her at her summer home in France, and that she knew about all of his sexual escapades there.

"Your mother shouldn't object to you meeting your father, Liz," was Uncle Joseph's reaction. "I'll have a talk with her."

Mom and Uncle Joseph did talk, and she agreed that now would be the appropriate time for me to meet my father. Mom and I developed a scheme. We would go downtown to the restaurant located across the street from the building in which Father had his office. This restaurant had large windows from which we could watch passersby. I hoped that we'd be able to see Father, if Mom could still recognize him after twenty years.

I was looking forward to having some of my lingering questions answered. I had such distressing thoughts as a child about my father. Why didn't he want me? Why had he never written or called me or in some way gotten in touch with me? Didn't he care at all? Now, finally, I'd get a glimpse of this stranger who had given me half of my genes. Would I see anything about him that I would also know about myself?

Soon the big day arrived. I found myself eating lunch at a table in Myer's Restaurant, peering out the window in search of my father. "Liz, that might be him over there. See that distinguished looking man with grey hair? But, I'm not sure. He's probably changed so much. I really don't know if I can recognize him.

"That's a good looking man, Mom," I replied. "But if you can't be sure, how we will we know?"

"I don't know, Liz."

We sat there another hour, until finally, I was discouraged. How could we be sure Father would walk by his office building that afternoon?

"Liz, maybe we could go to a nearby store and call your father. At least you might be able to talk to him over the phone."

"Okay, great!" I answered Mom. "Let's go do that."

****

"Emily! How good to hear from you. Is Elizabeth with you?" Father had answered the call after only a couple of rings.

"Yes, she's right here next to me," Mom replied. "We're at the phone booth in the drug store down the street."

"Both of you come over here. I want to meet my long-lost daughter!"

"All right," replied Mom. "We'll be over. What's your office number?"

We found his office, and before I could catch my breath, I was standing face to face with the father I'd never met but always wondered about.

"Elizabeth, what a beautiful young lady you are! Here I have a little something for you."

Father handed me a check for $200, which was a pleasant surprise. I knew he paid $35 per month in child support until I was thirteen and my grandfather died. I wondered if the missed child support payments motivated him to give me that check. I knew I could put it to good use, especially since Mario had sent me so little money.

Father went on, "My brother Jonathan and his wife Marianne are in town. I want you both to see them while they're here. How long will you both be here? Did you just arrive?"

"I've been here about six weeks, Father," I answered. "Mom just arrived a week ago, and we'll be here for a few more weeks. I wanted to wait until she was here to meet you, and now I'm glad we've finally met."

"So am I," he replied.

Father stood tall, at least six-foot-one. He was not as slender, nor as handsome as I'd remembered him in his pictures. However, he was pleasant in appearance for a man in his late fifties.

Father went on, "Let's drive over to the golf course and pick up Jonathan and Marianne. They're probably ready to come home by now. Then we can drive on down to Perrine and you can meet Joyce, my spouse. I want you both to meet her."

"I really feel that I should go on back to Joseph's," Mom said to him.

"But I want you to see my home and meet Joyce, Emily," Father replied enthusiastically.

"Well, then, you really should call your wife first," Mom cautioned.

"I'm sure she would not appreciate my coming to her home unannounced."

"I'll see," he replied.

I'd known Uncle Jonathan and Aunt Marianne since I was a child in Chicago. Evidently, Father forgot that. At any rate, I heard him saying to Uncle Jonathon as he walked up to meet him and Aunt Marianne, "Guess what? Elizabeth is here! Come on, I want you to meet my long-lost daughter!"

"Father, I don't need to be introduced to them," I said when they reached us. "I've known Uncle Jonathan and Aunt Marianne for years."

Aunt Marianne and Uncle Jonathan smiled, and we exchanged greetings. It was good to see two of the relatives I'd known in Chicago.

As we drove to Perrine, Aunt Marianne asked me, "Didn't we hear that you've just gotten married, Elizabeth?" She seemed concerned about my marital situation. She probably wondered where my new husband was during my visit in Miami.

"That's a terrible subject," I replied. "I'd just as soon not discuss it. We were married, and now we're separated. That's about it."

"And now you're pregnant, Elizabeth?"

"Yes," I replied. "That's the good part. I'm looking forward to being a mother."

"But it's a shame that your child won't have both a mother and a father."

"I know," I said, wanting to put an end to this discussion. "Please, let's talk about something else."

I was glad that there was no further discussion of my marriage.

Father's house was in Perrine, in southern Dade County, about a half hour's drive from downtown Miami. It didn't look as pretentious as I'd expected, having known the mansions I'd grown up with in Chicago. It did, however, have a large yard with an enclosed pool.

I don't remember meeting Joyce formally, although I'm sure that I must have. I do remember Father saying to her, somewhat to my surprise under the circumstances, "What do you think of my daughter, honey?"

"She's charming," Joyce responded, as she looked at me.

Several people huddled in Father and Joyce's living room. I sat next to a tall light fixture. I didn't realize that Uncle Jonathan sat on the other side of the light.

"I want to sit next to my lovely niece so I can get a good look at her. It sure has been a long time, Elizabeth."

That's the nicest compliment I've had in a long time, I thought. I didn't know he thought so much of me. We talked longer, and soon Father decided we should all go out to an Italian restaurant for dinner.

We sat around one huge table. Again Uncle Jonathan sat next to me, and again pleased me when he commented, "I never would have thought that my scoundrel brother could have such a lovely daughter. How did you manage it, Ken?"

"Elizabeth, looks more like her mother than like me, Jonathan," Father replied. "Can't you tell?"

"I think she looks more like you, Ken. But she's a lovely version of you!" Uncle Jonathan leaned over toward me and said more quietly, "You know, Elizabeth, your grandfather always favored you. Our brother Ed dotes over his grandchildren the way your grandfather doted over you."

I'd heard through the years from Mom how much Grandoo loved me, and I remembered how much he cared. But I was flattered by how much Uncle Jonathan stressed Grandoo's love for me.

Mom had also told me my grandoo was pleased that his son, whose own heritage was Scottish-English, had married a woman who also came from a good, Scottish-English family.

So, my first meeting with my father went quite successfully for both of us. Joyce was not pleased, however, which was expected. It must have been quite a shock for her to suddenly meet a step-daughter. She also wondered about Mother's motives. Would Ken's first wife try to win him back? Was this sudden meeting part of such an attempt?

I enjoyed my visit in Miami. Life was peaceful and happy. I loved to walk around Coconut Grove, where we visited various shops and ate lunch at quaint restaurants.

Occasionally, however, grim reality presented itself.

"Emily, this is Joyce, Kenneth's wife. I'm not at all happy that you and Elizabeth are here in Miami! If you two don't leave town, I will inform Elizabeth about how she was conceived. You wouldn't want her to know that, would you? So you'd better hurry and leave!"

"I'm sorry, Joyce," Mom replied. "But your threat won't work. Liz already knows all about the circumstances surrounding her birth!"

I had no idea Joyce was so angry toward Mom and me. Father told me that Joyce feared Mom was going to try and take him from her. Of course, we moved to Miami mainly because Uncle Joseph and Aunt Beth lived there, not for the reason Joyce feared.

A couple hours later, Father called to ask me what I knew about my birth. "Do you mean, Elizabeth, you already know that Emily and I weren't married when she became pregnant with you?"

"Yes," I replied. "It's no surprise. Mother told me all about it years ago. We're going to live in Iowa, anyway, so Joyce has no reason to fear."

We didn't leave Miami then, as Joyce had ordered.

Another unpleasant reality came in a letter from Mario. He enclosed a comic strip in which the hero was trying to get his wife to return to him. The character in the comic strip said, "The most important thing in the world to me is for my wife, the mother of my child, to return." Mario wrote that this was his goal, as well. Again, I was terribly confused. What right did Mario have to tear me apart this way? In the letter, he said he wanted me back again. If he wanted me as his wife and the mother of his child so badly, why had he suggested that we break up? Receiving this letter was very traumatic for me, and I cried.

Later the trauma was over, and I began to enjoy my experiences in Miami, with Mario out of my thoughts. I was looking forward to having my child. I got larger and larger, until I couldn't see my feet for my protruding stomach. I knew soon my baby would arrive.

Uncle Gerald and his family were vacationing in Hollywood, Florida. Uncle Joseph, his family, Mom, and I drove up to their motel to see them one Sunday. Uncle Gerald had mentioned to Mom that he could use her help in his nursing home that was located in Des Moines. Mom had been checking into Occupational Therapy programs in different nursing homes in Southern Florida in order to get ideas from good programs for Uncle Gerald's nursing homes in Iowa. Because Mom would be working for Uncle Gerald was the reason we planned to live in Iowa.

"You look great, Liz! Motherhood must agree with you." Aunt Phyllis seemed to be pleased with my healthy appearance.

"I do feel good," I replied. "Actually I can't remember when I've felt better!"

We had a pleasant visit with our three combined families. Then we returned to Miami, but not for long.

The train moved quickly up through Central and Northern Florida. I stood, staring down, but I could not see my feet. Then I looked over to the full-length mirror that hung from the door of our train compartment, and saw how fat and ugly I looked. God must not have been planning for beauty when he invented pregnancy, I decided. Thank goodness, my figure's not always this ugly.

The next day, we arrived in Memphis, where we got off the train and picked up Mom's car, which she had left there after fleeing from Carl. I'd never seen the Deep South before, with its red clay earth. We drove through several mountain communities, seeing people sitting in rocking chairs on their front porches. I had never seen country people or experienced southern culture before this trip.

One day, Mom and I were walking back to the car after eating breakfast in a restaurant. All of a sudden, a man whistled as he drove by. I was shocked. "Mom," I said in surprise, "I'm the only young woman he could have intended to whistle at, and I'm so pregnant!"

"I don't know, Hon," she answered. "Maybe he thinks pregnant women are beautiful."

That was a pleasant thought.

Chapter Nine

KENNY ARRIVES

Des Moines, 1961

When we arrived at Aunt Phyllis and Uncle Gerald's home in Iowa, they were still vacationing in Florida. The nanny, Mrs. Black, was supervising my cousins, who returned early for school. Mrs. Black's official bedtime was 9 p.m., but I rebelled at first, as it seemed too early. I wanted to sit up and read until 11. However, she was such a nice lady that I finally gave in and followed her rule. I decided it was probably for the best, since I would soon be going into the hospital.

After Aunt Phyllis and Uncle Gerald returned, Mom and I started looking for a place to live. We found a new duplex that we both liked and put down a deposit to hold it.

That same evening, right before dinner, I had pains in my stomach. I mentioned this to my aunt. She said that she doubted I was in labor, since my due date was two weeks away. She suggested I go ahead and eat dinner, regardless, so I did.

But the pains continued. At about 8 p.m., Uncle Gerald concluded that I was, indeed, in labor. He had me lie down. Aunt Phyllis lay down beside me. I found her gesture comforting because it displayed how much she cared. Aunt Phyllis was a nurse, and she had done quite a bit of nursing before she married, so I trusted her guidance and was happy I wasn't alone.

About 9 p.m., I lay in the hospital room being prepped. "My dear, are you sure you're in labor?" a nurse asked me. "You're so uncomplaining."

"That's what I'm told. I do have pain, but I'm trying not to yell." I had been praying that the Lord would be with me and help me not to yell.

****

The clock on the wall in the delivery room seemed to be moving so slowly. When would I be put to sleep? "Bear down, Liz," Uncle Gerald told me, "as though you're having a bowel movement." I did that five or six times.

"Oh!" I screamed, finally. This time the pain was too strong to remain silent. Still, I felt guilty and unhappy about releasing my screams.

"Hi, Elizabeth!" It was the anesthesiologist, who was sitting on a stool behind my head. "Just relax and breathe into this mask I'm putting over your nose and mouth." I was relieved. Since I'd never considered having natural childbirth, I was anxious to go to sleep and feel relief from the pain.

I started feeling woozy, but I was still aware of my surroundings. "She's a tall girl, isn't she, Gerald?" I heard the anesthesiologist say.

"All the women in our family are tall, Bill, as well as the men."

Here they are talking about me, thinking I won't hear them. Oh, well, at least they're saying something nice, I guess. After thinking this, I finally drifted off into a world of sleep and did not wake up again for quite a while.

****

"You've got a beautiful, healthy baby boy, Liz!"

I heard Uncle Gerald, but couldn't respond. I plunged back to sleep, aware of his good news.

"Didn't I hear Uncle Gerald tell me I had a boy?" I asked Mom when I finally awoke.

"That's right, Liz," she replied. "You'll probably be able to see him before long."

During my pregnancy, I'd been trying to decide on different boy's or girl's names for my child. The boy's name I selected was Kenneth Robert. I hadn't decided on a girl's name, so the task of naming my baby was simple, since he turned out to be a boy. Kenneth Robert it would be.

"What a beautiful baby!" I exclaimed when I first saw Kenny. He had long, dark hair, his complexion was somewhat dark, and he looked a little jaundiced. He also had a bump on his head, a hematoma, as they're called. I'd studied several baby books during my Miami visit, so the bump didn't scare me. The books all said hematomas were usually nothing to worry about with a newborn.

A couple of days later, I walked down the hall to the bathroom to take my first bath. Before reaching the bathroom, I stole a look at Kenny in the nursery.

He's such an adorable baby, I thought. I'll never be able to leave him to work, because I'll want to be with him. As I thought this, I knew that I would have to work in order to have the money to support him. Before Kenny was born, I had no idea the extent to which I would feel love for him. I was overwhelmed with the emotions I was feeling for him.

Things were going well. My baby was healthy and beautiful, and I felt well, considering what I'd just experienced. Things were going so well that I wasn't prepared for the next two problems which suddenly presented themselves. The nurse entering my room looked to be in her mid-twenties and was rather attractive. Her appearance did not prepare me for her rude question. "Were you married when you got pregnant?" she asked.

"Of course!" I snapped back. I felt fury at this woman's question. What was she trying to imply, that I had to get married because I was pregnant? Kenny was born two weeks early. I had not been married quite nine months when he was born, but that was because I'd become pregnant during our honeymoon. I had just had my period before the wedding. Another aspect of the nurse's question that bothered me was that Uncle Gerald was a practicing physician at that hospital, which made me wonder even more about her prying questions.

Good grief, I thought, a woman can't even marry, become pregnant right away, and then have a baby a little early without having people count the months suspiciously.

The second problem was that I had to face going through a divorce. But I also had an infant child whom I loved. I felt that somehow, with God's help, Kenny and I would get through it. Mom was also facing a divorce, but that had its positive aspects. I would no longer have to endure Carl's continuous verbally abusive assaults.

We were going to start anew in Iowa, Mom, Kenny, and I. Somehow, we would manage. We had paid the deposit on a duplex that we both really liked. Things seemed to be looking up, until Mom presented a new dilemma. This problem abruptly ended the positive, supportive emotional climate I'd experienced in Iowa. Instead, it set into motion a negative, disruptive climate.

"Liz, Gerald and I have been having some problems. He's had me really upset the last few days. I don't know if it's going to work out for us to live here, after all. I've been upset with all of this, but I haven't wanted to worry you." Mom looked older than usual, tired, and distressed, as she unburdened her heart to me there in my hospital room.

"But, Mom, where in this whole big world will we go?" All of a sudden, I felt fear. I hadn't even recuperated from giving birth, and I had to make this big decision with my mother, as to where in the country we would move to start our new life.

How can I decide and plan all of this right now? I wondered. I had just been able to relax, because I felt there was stability in my life. I had known much instability before, but I had placed high hopes in Mother's brothers, Joseph and Gerald. Mother had always told me how she and Gerald had been so close, and what a wonderful person he was. Wouldn't we be able to live in Iowa and look to his family to develop roots and stability?

My feelings of well-being dissolved. I no longer had a positive outlook about the return of strength to my body, and I desperately needed to be strong. It seemed as though I had struggled against events and people in my life for so long. Before, I'd "kept a stiff upper lip," and "turned the other cheek." I'd always come through my struggles, but I didn't know if I could cope any longer. I considered giving up.

But, evidently, some of my coping abilities still remained. "Mom, if we can't live here, I think we should go back to California. One very good reason to go there is that will be where yours and Carl's divorce with be handled. It would be to your advantage to be there for the divorce proceedings."

"What about our living in Miami?" Mom replied. "Remember, Joseph told us before we left that if we ever felt we'd like to live near his family in Miami, we'd be welcome."

"Yes, I know Mom," I answered. "But for right now I think priority should be given to protecting you during your divorce. You wouldn't want Carl to claim desertion, and have him win the divorce because you're not there to state your case as to why you left him. He'd come out with everything, and you with nothing." We decided that our next home would be California, temporarily.

Two days later, I left the hospital and returned to Uncle Gerald's home. Mom told me that Kenny would need to be two months old before he could travel, so we would stay in Iowa until then and afterward drive to California. Our stay at Uncle Gerald's was not always pleasant. It was evident that there was discord between Mom and her brother, although Aunt Phyllis did her best to help their relationship.

I nursed Kenny in the beginning, but before long, I became aware that I wasn't up to it physically. I was tired all the time. I would lie down several times during the day as a retreat from the constant demands of feedings, bathing, washing, as well as my growing inner turmoil and discouragement. Why am I so tired? I wondered. I felt well during my pregnancy, and now I just can't seem to keep up physically with all the demands. One day, a friend of Aunt Phyllis said to me, "Liz, you look anemic. Are you sure you should be nursing Kenny? Maybe you should ask your uncle about bottle-feeding him instead."

"I wanted to succeed with breast-feeding him," I said sadly. "But I sure haven't been feeling well."

Uncle Gerald agreed that I would probably feel better if I discontinued feeding Kenny myself and used bottle feedings, so I stopped breastfeeding him.

Soon Kenny was old enough for the long drive to California. We collected our belongings and packed everything into Mom's chevy.

"If I can ever help you in anyway, Liz, just let me know. I'll always be here for you."

I wondered about what Uncle Gerald had just said to me. I couldn't help but think that this comment was somewhat strange under the circumstances. Mother and I both had come to Uncle Gerald specifically for help, but now we had to leave.

Life is so full of problems sometimes, I thought. Even when people sincerely try to help each other, their attempts often fail. Well, anyway, he says he'll always be willing to help me with any problems I might have. At least that's good to know. I may take him up on his offer one day. His gesture eased some of my anguish over his and Mom's difficulties. They must have had a communication problem with each other or something, I decided. I'm sure neither one of them consciously wanted to hurt the other.

I thought back to the time when Mom had picked Uncle Gerald as my guardian, if anything were to happen to her. That had been his wish. I must have been seven or eight years old the day we went to a lawyer's office in Seattle, and Uncle Gerald was officially designated as my guardian. I felt strange that day, wondering why Mom worried about something happening to her. Nothing would happen to her, would it? I wondered that day in Seattle. As I was growing up, I always received a big Christmas check from Uncle Gerald and Aunt Phyllis, and felt blessed that they cared so much.

As I stood that day in Iowa with my uncle, I recalled a month or so before when I sat on Mom's bed and looked up at him. He said, with obvious distress, "There're so many people I'm helping. I can't help everyone with everything! I'm just one person."

Uncle Gerald had several health problems, the worst of which was a serious heart condition. As I said goodbye to him and his family, I realized that we are all so humanly fragile. Maybe I can't lean on him, I thought. Perhaps people are leaning on him too much already.

Mom, Kenny, and I would need to find our new life somewhere else.

Chapter Ten

TWO DIVORCES, ONE YEAR

Los Angeles, 1961

The trip was miserable. It was very hot in summer through the midwestern states and in California. There was much work to do, caring for Kenny. Even simple baby care tasks were difficult to perform while riding for many miles in our cramped car. At night we took everything out of the car and into the motel room, and then the following morning we would pack everything back into the car before continuing our journey. Mom was the only one with a driver's license, so we had to rely completely upon her for the long trek between Iowa and California.

We went first to Northern California. When we arrived in San Jose, we were impressed with the city. We thought it might be a nice place to settle down.

We'd be further away from Carl there than in Los Angeles, and we'd be close to Seattle if we wanted to visit our family and friends there occasionally.

One day, shortly after we arrived in San Jose, Mom decided to call Carl at our home in Redondo Beach to determine the status of their separation. She had heard from our minister, Rev. Miller, while we were in Iowa. He'd written that Carl had been attending church and that he was quite "repentant." He also wrote that Carl had been profoundly affected by Mom leaving. Also, Carl had sent Mom a beautiful bouquet for Mother's Day, and I'd received a bouquet and a card from Carl when Kenny was born. That was a "warm fuzzy" for me. Carl had never given me a present before. His thoughtfulness was a positive happening at the time of Kenny's birth. Mom wanted to find out what her next move should be.

"Could I speak to Carl, please?" Mom asked when Grandma Jones answered the phone.

"No, you can't speak to him, Emily," she replied. "He isn't here right now. If you have anything to tell him, you'll have to say it to his lawyer."

We were surprised to learn that Carl's parents had come to California. Mom decided we should go to

Los Angeles so she could find herself a lawyer and be closer to their home in Redondo Beach. We rented a furnished apartment in southern Los Angeles. It had been my idea when we were in Iowa that Mom and I would be "roommates" after my child's birth and our divorces.

I believed that if I were to have a roommate my age, she probably wouldn't be able to put up with a small child, and Kenny's and my life would remain unstable. I feared I would often have to find a roommate that could get along with a divorced mother and her baby. Since Mom and I got along well together, we could provide more stability for all of us. And, I'd have some help with the raising of my child, at least until I might meet someone to remarry. Neither Mom nor I had much money, and we didn't have hope of receiving very much in the way of financial help from either Carl or Mario. So, we also hoped sharing expenses would ease our financial burden.

I still felt a pull to be at home with my baby. I worked hard cleaning our apartment, taking Kenny for walks, and caring for his needs. He was a plump, adorable baby. He looked Italian with his olive complexion, dark eyes, and dark hair.

Although I kept busy working, I couldn't help feeling increasing despair. I dreaded the months to come while we would be awaiting the divorce proceedings. I wondered if I could maintain my sanity through it all. I found I was getting more irritable with Mom, although I was not that way with Kenny. He was such a good baby; he seldom provoked me. Mom was patient and understanding. I decided she must be much stronger than I emotionally. She found a job and told me that working was helping her keep her mind off her problems.

One Sunday morning, I lay in bed reading the newspaper. Mom was in the next bed, also reading. As I lay there, I thought about the fact that I hadn't finished college and that I probably never would be able to go back. All of a sudden, I burst out crying.

"Mom," I said, sobbing, "I always thought I would graduate from college. Now I'll probably never be able to go back. I won't be able to afford it. It's just so depressing because I always assumed I'd make it through college. Now all I face is years of working and housecleaning, and without a husband and father for my child."

"Liz, you married before you finished college, so maybe you married too young." In my state of mind, I hadn't considered that fact. I just felt depressed, without applying any logic or common sense. Mom had been very positive about my returning to college the year after I quit Trinity. She'd suggested that I attend one of the California state colleges that were so highly acclaimed. But I had my heart set on going to a Christian College. I didn't want to attend any "secular" school, I'd decided. I investigated Pepperdine College, which was a Christian College, but found out that, even though I would be accepted, I couldn't afford to go there unless I worked. I didn't think I could physically cope with working my way through another year of college. Consequently, I didn't continue with my education; I'd married Mario. That day in our apartment, I felt despair and defeat at not having completed college as I'd always dreamed.

Mom was working in Redondo Beach, quite a drive every day. We decided to move closer to her work. We found a small, furnished apartment in Hermosa Beach. We didn't expect to stay there long, just until Mom's divorce proceedings were over.

I hadn't been feeling well physically, as well as emotionally. I went to see Dr. Williams, Mom's former boss. After examining me and running some tests, he told me I had a vaginal infection called Trichomoniasis and a kidney infection. He prescribed medicine I needed for the kidney infection, but was unable to give me any medicine for the vaginal infection because it was only available in Canada.

I was gradually becoming more and more of a semi-invalid, physically from the infections, but even more, mentally from my growing emotional ill health. I did only what I had to do around the apartment. I cared for Kenny's immediate needs and that was about it. The rest of the time I lay around watching television, with Kenny in his playpen nearby. A couple times I did try to complete some housework, in an attempt to help clean up the mess. But I always ended up taking rests, after doing some small task, so I didn't accomplish much. Mom did most of the housework I should have been doing in the evenings after she returned from work. I blamed my lethargy on my physical condition.

Dr. Williams told me I could get a job and work if I just would, because I was not too ill to work. But

I was not even functioning well enough to take care of my household responsibilities, so I didn't see how I could work.

"I feel you should see someone about your other problem, Liz," Dr. Williams said to me one day over the phone.

"What 'other problem'?" I snapped back.

"I'm referring to your emotional problem, Liz."

"I don't have any emotional problem! I'm just fine," I replied.

But I was becoming more of a recluse. I hardly ever went outside or took advantage of living so near the beach. I didn't realize that I my extreme lack of energy and motivation were due to developing emotional problems.

"I'd like you to see a doctor at the U.C.L.A Medical Center." Dr. Williams continued. "I'll set up an appointment for you. All right?"

"If you can help me get over the infections so I won't be so tired, I'll go." I did want to feel better and have more energy, so I let him set up an appointment.

I wondered if it was the vaginal infection that was making me feel so terrible. I called Mario and told him I had Trichomoniasis; he claimed I had gotten it from another man. Typical of Mario to deny every-thing, but I knew better. Fortunately, Mother was able to locate a doctor in Canada that she once knew, and he was able to mail the medicine to me, which cleared up the vaginal infection.

I kept my appointment at the U.C.L.A Medical Center, but apparently the doctors there didn't rec-ognize that I was having symptoms of poor mental health and needed treatment. Several of them talked to me. Nothing ever developed, however, as a treatment plan for anything other than my infections. Evidently, even though I was suffering emotionally, it was not that apparent to others at that time.

A lot of my problems were caused by my con-tinuing dread about Mom and Carl's court proceed-ings that would be happening soon. As the dreaded day approached, I worried about getting on the wit-ness stand and testifying. I also dreaded facing the confrontation with Carl. I knew I would have to listen to more accusations from him as to what an awful person I was, and how I'd tried to break up his and Mom's marriage. I didn't know if I could stand more accusations, especially in front of everyone in the courtroom.

****

"If your life was so terrible with Carl Jones, then why did you stay married to him for thirteen years, Mrs. Jones?" It was the day of the divorce proceedings. The attorney Mom had hired appeared to be trying to understand just what the situation had been with Carl, Mom, and me. As I stood in the courtroom that day in January, 1962, I felt I had to defend Mom and answer her lawyer's probing question.

"Because she's such a good Christian," I told him firmly. "She doesn't take divorce lightly." He looked at both of us with a puzzled expression on his face, but didn't ask anything further.

I'd seen Grandma and Grandpa Jones sitting together shortly after we arrived. I went up to them and sat down. "Hi! Good to see you!"

Grandma didn't seem to be sure how to respond to my greeting, but she was polite. The three of us sat and talked for a while as we waited for the judge to come in and start proceedings. I glanced at Mother a couple of times, wondering if she would be hurt by my sitting with "the other side," but she didn't look particularly concerned. I decided that, after all,

Mother was broad-minded enough that this small situation wouldn't trouble her. It was important to me to have the good will of my step-grandparents. They had always been good to me, and I loved both of them.

But, once again, as I'd done when I met my father in Miami earlier, I was repressing the strong feelings I was having at this climactic event. Rather than trying to deal with those emotions, I was sitting next to Grandma and Grandpa, discussing trivialities. I only knew I didn't want to be their enemy. It seemed to me that they acted as though they had similar feelings.

Carl was noticeably upset as he answered questions. He spoke wildly and incoherently. When I was in the witness chair, I felt strange. I wanted to be kind to Carl, but I also knew that I had to honestly recount what happened in our home all the years he and Mom were married. As I answered the lawyers and judge's questions, I felt detached from what I was saying, as though a part of me was saying the words, but the rest of my personality couldn't cope with what I was going through emotionally.

Finally, it was over, and Mom was awarded the divorce. Her lawyer told us that before we'd all been on the witness stand, he wasn't too sure if we would win. But, he said, after seeing Carl's erratic behavior, both he and Carl's lawyer had realized that we were the injured parties. Carl was the one at fault.

I wanted to say goodbye to Carl and wish him well before we left the courthouse. When Mom was saying goodbye to him in the parking lot, I found an opportunity to say, "Carl, I want to wish you the best of everything." I reached out my hand to shake his.

Ignoring my outstretched hand, he replied, "I don't ever want to see you again!"

His words hit hard. I was still hoping for friendship with Carl, even then, and he cut me down instead. Oh well, I thought, I guess there just isn't any hope for friendship or kindness from him. I'd be better off forgetting about it.

Mom and I once again had a decision to make as to where we would live. I remembered my good feelings in Miami with Uncle Joseph and his family. I told Mom that I thought we'd be the happiest there. By this time, she wasn't as sure as I was that Miami was the best place for us. She pointed out how far Florida was from California, and that the move would probably cost so much money we wouldn't have much left afterwards. The couple of thousand dollars she would receive when the Redondo Beach home sold and the money divided between her and Carl would probably just cover moving. Once again, we'd have financial difficulties.

Mom had not asked for alimony from Carl. She knew he made a very small salary, and she was concerned about his welfare without her. He'd told her when they were married, that if she ever left him, he'd "take a little black pill." She planned to make her own money without handicapping Carl. Yet, although Mom was concerned about the financial burden of a move to Florida, she wanted to consider my wishes in this decision as well as her own.

We also considered moving to Seattle, near our relatives there. But I was afraid of living that close to Carl. It scared me to think about possible harassment. Although, in many ways the thought of being near old friends in Seattle and Kenniltown appealed to me, I also realized that there would probably be many conversations about Mom and Carl's divorce. I would also continually be reminded of Carl's and my bad relationship. I wanted to get far away from Carl and all the things that reminded me of him.

We called Aunt Beth and Uncle Joseph and told them we might be returning to Miami, that we might take Uncle Joseph up on his offer to live near them. They told us that if we did return to Miami, we should feel free to stay with them until we located a place of our own. We did decide to move to Miami.

For a woman who hadn't driven much before these last four or five years, Mom was courageous in her accomplishments. First, she had driven from California to Memphis. Then she drove from Memphis to Iowa and from Iowa to California. Now, she planned to drive from California to Florida. I decided Mom must have a lot of guts.

Before the three of us left for Florida, we made one last visit to our Hollywood Riviera, Redondo Beach home. The Jones were staying there while in the process of selling the house.

This visit went well. Kenny was nine months old by then, and one of the cutest babies around. I looked at Kenny while we talked with Carl and his parents, and prayed, thank you, God, that my son will not have to experience the trauma I went through at Carl's hands. It's been hard going through Mom's divorce with her, but now I am very thankful that Kenny will have a chance at the life he deserves.

****

Soon after reaching Miami, we found a house to rent on one of the main streets in Coconut Grove. Our antique furniture fit right in. I enjoyed picking flowers from our yard and placing them in my antique sugar shaker for a centerpiece on our "new," second-hand, wrought-iron table.

It didn't take me long to find a job. My very first full-time job was with Apex Insurance Agency in downtown Miami, located near the section of town where many Cuban families were setting up businesses. I was a secretary. Mom also obtained a job, in a medical office.

Soon, I called Father to let him know that Mom, Kenny and I were back in Miami, this time to make our home here.

"I don't want Joyce to know you're here," Father said. "We'll get together you and I, without letting her know."

Father and I went to lunch together once a week, and he also took me to movies.

One afternoon, Father took me to a theater in Miami Beach to see *Thoroughly Modern Millie*. Father parked his Cadillac, and then he surprised me when he looked at me and said, "You know, Liz, on an island in the Mediterranean, fathers and daughters have sex with each other."

Shocked, I jumped in my seat and loudly replied, "I don't do anything like that!" Nothing more was said about that, and we went to the movie theater and enjoyed Mary Tyler Moore, the star. Life went on, and this topic never came up again. The episode did have an effect on my mind, though, because I remembered all the warnings we received about Father's sexual behaviors. The statement he made didn't help my emotional condition.

****

At work everyone praised me for learning their insurance plans so quickly and being such a good typist. I did have some difficulties, however. I continued to work full time, but I didn't seem to have much energy left after work.

In the mornings, Mom would have to do most of the work of getting Kenny ready to go to the babysitter's home a couple of miles away. Then, since I was taking the bus to work and Mom was driving, she would drive Kenny to and from the babysitter's. Often Mom would complain that I should do more of Kenny's care in the mornings. My reply was, "It's all I can do to get ready and go to work. I don't think I can accomplish anything more."

I felt a certain amount of pressure from Mom and our relatives to accomplish more, but I really couldn't do all that was expected of me. I was finding it hard enough to function well enough to make it to work.

Neither Mario nor I had yet filed for divorce. Since Father was an attorney, I went to see him for advice. I knew I needed money from Mario for Kenny. Father suggested that I look into Uniform Support for Dependents. He said that I wouldn't even have to be divorced for the Department of State Attorney's Office to help us.

The woman who was in charge of Uniform Support for Dependents was very cooperative. She said she would write to Missouri immediately, so that, in case Mario filed for divorce soon, my petition would reach the judge before his. I had not had residency anywhere since leaving Missouri, so it hadn't been possible for me to file for divorce. However, we received word from Missouri that Mario had filed for divorce, and that his petition had reached the judge first.

Time passed. Kenny had his first birthday in May, 1962, and my petition came to a hearing twice. But each time, Mario's lawyer asked the judge to postpone the case, saying Mario preferred to handle the child support agreement through the divorce rather than though my Uniform Support for Dependents' petition.

Father expressed concern that I was asking for too much money from Mario. The petition asked for $40 per week. Father also felt the divorce proceedings would be the preferred way of handling the child support. He suggested I ask for no more than $100 per month. He said that it was better to ask for less and get it regularly, than to ask for more and not receive it.

I spoke to the woman who was handling my petition at Uniformed Support for Dependents and told her Father's feelings. She disagreed. She said the petition through her office would have a much better chance of being effective, that, when it went through, any time Mario didn't make a payment he would have to pay or face jail.

I guess my father's influence was greater on me than that of the woman at the State Attorney's Office. Since I wasn't functioning well then, I just wanted to get the divorce over with. I agreed to take Father's counsel. I wrote a letter relinquishing my rights under Uniform Support, which I had to do to end my petition. Having written that, Mario's and my divorce soon went through. Mario claimed I'd deserted him, but Father wrote my case explaining what had transpired during our brief marriage. Even though the judge didn't hear my case directly from me, Father obtained a good lawyer in St. Louis who stated the case as it honestly was, and I was awarded the divorce.

Finally, both traumatic divorces were over. I wondered if I finally would be able to regain my emotional health. Perhaps my new environment would heal my emotional wounds, and my life could begin anew.

Chapter Eleven

THE EMERGENCE OF INSANITY

Miami/Des Moines, 1962

By now, I was beginning to learn more about Father's ancestors. One evening, Father and I ate dinner at a local restaurant. When we stood up from the table to leave, Father said to me, "Liz, I don't know if you are aware of this, but you are a sixth great-granddaughter of Samuel Adams."

Hearing that I thought, I already know that I'm a descendant of John Adams, so I guess they were related.

Father continued, "Sam was John Adams's second cousin. You've probably heard of the Boston Tea Party, back during the American Revolution. Sam was behind that revolt. He is considered the 'Father of the American Revolution.'"

My mind was not helping me as much as it had before, but it registered this new interesting fact. I didn't say anything.

A week later, Father and I stood on a pier overlooking Biscayne Bay when he said, "You know, Liz, your mother and I had only a casual relationship when she became pregnant with you." Although I knew that what he said wasn't true, I didn't say anything in response. Hearing those words was a terrible blow to me. Mom had told me many times that they had dated for at least a year, and I believed her. With all that was happening, I was struggling to stay in my right mind.

It was too late, however. I was caught in the gradual process of descent into a deep, dark fantasy world. During the period since Kenny's birth, when both divorces were being contested, my main symptoms had been fatigue, worry, and feelings of not being able to cope with life and function normally. I was now receding into myself. My thinking processes had changed, becoming distorted. As a friend of mine at work pointed out, "Liz, you sure do have a good imagination!" Yes, my imagination was improving, but not in a healthy manner. Reality was becoming less and less clear, and deranged thinking was setting in.

****

"You know, Liz, there are lots of homosexuals living in Coconut Grove, where you live," stated one of my managers at work, as he looked at me somewhat curiously in anticipation of my response.

"I didn't know that," I replied. Homosexuals, I thought, just what does that mean? I know that is some sort of sexual behavior, but what do they do?

I thought back to my school years. Those of us who wore a certain color on a certain day of the week were labeled "faeries." Was homosexual another term for what we called "faerie?" Does he think I'm a homosexual because I live in Coconut Grove? I wondered. He must. But, I'm not even sure what it's all about, so how can I be one? The world must be going crazy if people think I'm a homosexual. I bet everyone else here at Apex suspects me of being that way.

Then one day, a female co-worker, Julie, asked me about my relationship with my husband. When I told her about Mario making me have sex with him from behind and in the wrong opening, she said, "Liz, what he did to you was sodomy. He could be arrested for

191

that!" I really didn't want Mario to have to go to jail, so I made a note of what she said, but forgave Mario.

However, making it to work was getting harder and harder each day. Before long, I was only able to make it there some days. I had to rest all of the time I was at home, and I wouldn't go out in the evenings or on weekends. I was lethargic and spent most of my time lying on the couch. Soon winter came, and we had no heat other than one or two small heaters. I caught a cold, and couldn't make it to work at all.

At the time of the emergence of my fantasies, the Cuban Missile Crisis was the pressing national issue. This fact only added fuel to my imaginary framework. The end of the world must be coming very soon, I thought, as I lay on our antique couch watching television. The Communists want us all to become homosexuals so they can weaken our country and overtake it. That must be where the homosexuals fit in. Well, I just won't cooperate, that's all.

When I did make it back to the office, strange happenings were going on there. Mr. Thompson, my boss, was interviewing a woman for a job. Was it for my job? If it was, why hadn't he told me I was being "let go" before he began looking for a new secretary?

Strange, really strange, I thought. But then, isn't my world made up only of strange? My secretarial job lasted approximately nine months. "We feel you need a good rest to get yourself together, Liz. Probably the divorces and all that you've been through recently were very traumatic and you haven't fully recovered. We think you may need to be rehabilitated. Mr. Whitehall was my boss's superior, and I'd always liked him. He seemed that day to be his usual pleasant self.

"Rehabilitated," I murmured. "That must be what I need. Maybe I need to be rehabilitated." I occasionally sensed all was not right in my head. Mr. Whitehall had called me into his office, along with Mr. Thompson, my boss, and gently let me go.

A couple of weeks later, I heard these words, "Goodbye, Liz. Hope things work out for you."

Everyone seemed nice the day I left Apex for the last time. But they must have other motives, I thought. If they're so nice, then why are they firing me?

****

"Maybe you shouldn't worry about working for a while, Liz. Beth and I have been talking, and we feel maybe you should just take care of Kenny and not worry about work." Mom seemed concerned about my health. Yes, it would be a relief not to work for a while. I simply stayed home after that.

Aunt Beth and I went to a luncheon at the church one day shortly after I left Apex. As we walked through Coconut Grove after lunch, she asked me if I thought I had emotional problems. She said that maybe I should consider seeing a doctor.

Why does everyone say I'm having emotional problems? I thought. Why doesn't she just leave me alone? "I'm fine, Aunt Beth," was my response. "After my year at Bible College I had emotional problems, but that's all over now."

One day at our home I was busy preparing dinner for Uncle Joseph and his family, and our good friend, Yvonne and her family. While I was cleaning, washing clothes, and otherwise getting things ready, I had a powerful foreboding feeling about the return of Christ in the Rapture that I had learned about. I looked out our kitchen window, in anticipation that at any moment I would see Jesus coming in the sky.

All of a sudden, I was worried about all of our family on Mother's side. I didn't know whether they were all Christians, so right then I prayed for Mom's sister, her brothers, and for their families, that if they were not saved they would be in time for the fulfillment of biblical prophecy. Then I remembered that somewhere in the Gospels of the New Testament, it was written that two persons will be together, doing various tasks and one will be taken, the other one left. Does this mean, I wondered, if I'm with Mom or Kenny when the Rapture occurs, that only one of us will be taken? I can't let that happen. All three of us are Christians, so we all must go with Him. What will I do?

Then I realized that Kenny hadn't ever been baptized. It occurred to me that maybe I could baptize him, since I was a Christian and I'd attended a Bible college. I picked up Kenny and took him to our bathroom, where I sprinkled water onto his head. Then I thought, now he's ready for the Lord.

Night approached, our dinner guests arrived, ate, conversed and later went home, yet all I could think about was that Christ did not come. I decided it must not be the time. My mind raced wildly from one disjointed thought to the next.

I couldn't sleep that night. I was afraid, afraid of Mother, who lay in the other twin bed only a few feet from me. She's going to kill me, I thought. She'll probably go out in the kitchen, get a butcher knife, and bring it back here and stab me. I'll defend myself, though, somehow. I'm not going to let her kill me. As I lay there, my thoughts changed content constantly. I remained alert, however, to any threat Mom might pose.

If only I'd cried when Grandfather died, I thought. Then I wouldn't have the problems I have now. But what problems do I have, anyway? Sometimes I would think they're all right; I am mentally Ill. That's an awful thought. If I am mentally Ill, they'll put me in an asylum in chains. How awful. I won't let them put me there. I'll go to someone who'll help me, who'll keep me from the people who want to put me away. I know, I'll go to the church. I'll leave soon, get in the sanctuary, and sleep in a pew until our minister gets there in the morning. Then I'll tell him about all the terrible things that are happening, how Mom wants to kill me, and people want to put me away. He'll help me.

Something's strange. All of the sudden, it seems like Satan is trying to talk to me. He's saying that he wants me to marry him and he wants me to have his baby. How could I ever want to get involved with Satan, even if he could offer me the whole world? No, sorry, Satan, I'm not interested. Go find someone else to have your fun with.

My thoughts returned to my problem of escape. Maybe it would be better if I went to Iowa instead of to the church. Uncle Gerald offered his help if I ever need it, so I could take him up on his offer now. Yes, it would be safe there. Uncle Gerald would never do anything to hurt Kenny or me.

I did sleep a couple of hours that morning. Then, after Mom went to work, I started getting some of Kenny's and my clothes together for the trip to Iowa. I had finally decided that would be where we would go. Holding Kenny's small hand, I walked into our bank to close out my account in order to have money for the train. Boy, the people in here look strange, I thought, as I prepared my checkbook to take to a cashier. I'll have to make sure they don't find out that I'm leaving town, because they might contact Mom or Aunt Beth and Uncle Joseph. They're looking at me like they think I'm strange. I'd better act my best so I don't arouse too much suspicion. I completed the closing of my account and led Kenny out of the bank and back to our house, which was within walking distance. I felt somewhat relieved and thought, I guess we made it through that all right. But, now we've got the whole trip ahead of us to Des Moines, Iowa. I'll have to be very cautious for the entire trip.

It was late afternoon when our train left. By then, my paranoid structure had become even more complex. I found myself thinking, Mom isn't the only person who wants me dead. Several people right here on this train also want to kill me. I know why, too. Right now there is a Communist invasion going on in the United States. I'd better watch out for the people in the seat behind me, because they will kill me if I give them a chance.

I looked outside to the countryside we were passing. Everything I saw seemed to fit with my weird thoughts. No wonder there are so many people coming and going from those buildings out there, I thought. It's all part of the great Communistic plot. They're killing the Americans and taking over their jobs. It won't be long before the whole United States will be overtaken by them. World War III will soon be upon us.

All of a sudden, I realized that neither Kenny nor I had eaten since breakfast. I decided I'd better get some food, especially for him. I wasn't very hungry myself.

"Are you and your little boy going for dinner?" I turned in the direction of the voice, and saw a handsome young man, my age or a little younger.

"Yes, we are."

"Mind if I join you?" He asked.

"Of course not," I replied.

We had dinner, Kenny and I on one side of the small table, and the young man on the other side. He seemed quite interested in getting to know me, but my mind was so scrambled that I was in no shape to reciprocate. He wanted to pay for our meals, but I wouldn't let him. I knew that meals on trains were terribly expensive, too expensive for a young man to pay for three meals, especially when I was hardly talking to him. Finally, after we ate and returned to our seats, the fellow either realized I was behaving strangely, or I succeeded in discouraging him, because he didn't talk with me any further.

The next day we reached the Chicago train station. I don't remember how long we waited before we got on the train for Des Moines, but it must have been at least two or three hours. It certainly seemed that long.

Kenny was a toddler, and, as toddlers will, he ran all over the Chicago station. I ran after him, and it seemed as though I was constantly running. Who will know where Kenny is if I lose him? I thought. Mom has no idea where we are. How could she or anyone know where he is? I was a crazy woman running after her son, and reprimanding him verbally for being "naughty." Running after Kenny was not my sole preoccupation that day, as all-consuming as it was physically. Mentally, I was working just as hard. I stood in the ladies' room, looking around at the other women. I thought to myself that there were many Communists there, too. I decided the sooner we made it to Uncle Gerald's home, the better.

When we arrived in Des Moines, I noticed the snow. Living in California and Florida, I'd almost forgotten that it does snow in the winter. Therefore, I hadn't brought the right clothes. It was late at night, so rather than bother Aunt Phyllis and Uncle Gerald, I took Kenny and went to a hotel in town.

By the time I walked into our hotel room, I was scared. I was afraid that all the Communists who were out to get us would find us. But, I thought, still in the grip of fear, maybe we'll be safe here for tonight. Exhausted, I collapsed on the bed and fell asleep. I didn't do much for Kenny that night, or for that matter, the next morning.

We took a cab to our family's home in Des Moines the next morning. When I saw Uncle Gerald and Aunt Phyllis, I realized their concern for us. I felt a warm feeling, as if they cared. Indeed, help was there for Kenny and me. I told them everything.

"We'd like you to meet a doctor friend of ours, Liz." Uncle Gerald smiled as he spoke. "You can tell him all those things you've been telling us about your fears. He'll be very understanding, and he can help you."

"Why don't you get cleaned up, Liz, take a bath and put on some fresh clothes?" Aunt Phyllis also spoke warmly. I was puzzled as I sat in the bathtub, but I wanted to cooperate with my loving aunt and uncle.

Soon we were riding in Uncle Gerald's Cadillac until we reached a brick building. Following my aunt and uncle, I walked into a section of the building, wondering where we were going, but trusting and believing in my relatives' judgment.

"Liz, this is the psychiatric wing of Blythe Memorial Hospital. It's new, and we're very proud of it." Uncle Gerald showed me the entire wing, and I was impressed. Later, one of the young male attendants told me that when he saw my uncle and me walking through that day, he had no idea I was being admitted as a psychiatric patient. He thought I was someone looking the place over, a professional. Indeed, that day I did have the feeling that I was being shown Blythe Hospital's Psychiatric Wing as a matter of interest and enrichment. What a fantasy world I was in.

Then a fragment of reality set in. Uncle Gerald and Aunt Phyllis took me to a rather small room with two beds and not much else. "This will be your room at first, Liz." Aunt Phyllis seemed to be trying to speak in a non-threatening way. I realized then that I was to be a psychiatric patient, after all.

"But what about Kenny, Aunt Phyllis?" I asked anxiously. "Where will he be? Won't I be able to have him with me?"

"He'll be at home with us, Liz. Don't worry, we'll take good care of him. Our children will help care for him. They also love Kenny, as you and I do."

"All right," I said, still trusting and reassured that Kenny would be all right.

A woman passed by my room with a cart. She had books, candy, gum, perfume, and other such items for all of us on the ward. "Hello, would you like to check out a library book or buy something?," she asked.

"No thanks," I answered. "I don't think I can read a book right now. Maybe another time."

"Okay, I come by each afternoon, so just let me know when you see me." The woman seemed friendly and kind.

"You'll be able to get plenty of sleep here, Liz," Aunt Phyllis commented.

"I feel like I could use lots of sleep. I guess that will be good for me."

"You know, Liz, some psychiatrists believe that sleep is a very important medicine for mental illness.

In some countries right now doctors are attempting to cure their patients by having them sleep a lot."

"Maybe it helps," I said.

"Well, I guess we'd better be going. The doctors and nurses will take good care of you. Uncle Gerald and I will try to visit you whenever we can. Goodbye."

"Goodbye," I replied. I wondered what it was going to be like living in Blythe Psychiatric Wing.

A short time later, an aide told me that I was to see Dr. Cummings.

"Who's he?" I queried.

"He's going to be your doctor, Elizabeth. You'll like him. He's awfully nice."

We reached Dr. Cummings's office. The aide opened the door and introduced me to him. Indeed, he did look like a nice man. Good, I thought, I can tell him about all the things that are going on in my life. He certainly doesn't look like a Communist.

"Dr. Cummings, I've been going through the most awful Hell. My mother was going to kill me, so I left my home with my son and came up here to Des Moines in order to save my life. But, on the way here, the Communists began invading the United States, and several of them wanted to kill me."

It was a relief to finally unburden myself to this kindly man. "Elizabeth, I think you've been through some traumatic experiences in your life, and now you're experiencing some emotional problems." Dr. Cummings did not seem threatening as he spoke.

"You mean I'm mentally ill?" I asked, wondering if my worst suspicions had actually been correct, that all of this I was experiencing was insanity.

"Not mentally ill, Elizabeth," he replied. "I would call it emotional difficulty."

This explanation was comforting, especially since it was now evident that I was not going to be chained and beaten, as I dreaded that sleepless night in Miami. Could he be right? I wondered. Could I be emotionally disturbed? Maybe he is right, I don't know. At least I feel I can trust this doctor. He will be a good person to talk to.

The next day I was transferred to the ward for "improved" patients. I was also taken to a doctor's office in the hospital for a physical examination. He's going to find out that I'm pregnant, I thought, all the while the doctor examined me. I didn't know why I believed this crazy thought, because I had not had any sexual relations since I had been with Mario, but I was very sure that must have been why he was doing a pelvic examination. Then, when the doctor did not tell me I was pregnant, this disjointed, crazy thought left my bewildered mind as quickly as it had appeared.

Soon I started going to therapies. In the mornings I went to Occupational Therapy; then in the afternoons I was in Recreation Therapy. If I proved myself to be a really good patient, I would be able to have a pass to leave the hospital and walk over to the shopping center across the street by simply signing myself out and back in.

My first morning in Occupational Therapy, Aunt Phyllis and Uncle Gerald came to visit. "We've received such good reports about your behavior, Liz. You shouldn't have to be in here long if you keep doing so well." Aunt Phyllis beamed as she told me the good news.

"Kenny is doing fine, too," Uncle Gerald said. "Every night right at 8:00 o'clock he gets up on my lap to let me know it's his bed time."

As for what I was experiencing and feeling during this discussion, my main preoccupation was trying to decide whether I would live or die. I'd had a cold when I was admitted to the hospital. I was feeling such strange feelings in my head that morning in Occupational Therapy. I thought I definitely must be dying from pneumonia. Other than that, I was somewhat pleased at my aunt and uncle's apparent happiness and pleasure with my progress. But, for the most part, I just wanted to talk to Dr. Cummings about all the prickly, weird feelings centered in my head.

Later that morning, I did get a chance to talk to him. "I think it's just the side effects of the medicine called Stelazine that I've given you. That's what is making you feel those strange feelings. If they're bothering you, I'll cut the dosage in half."

Then I'm not dying of pneumonia, I thought. What a relief. Dr. Cummings cut the dosage in half, and the prickly feelings subsided.

That afternoon, I decided to check out a book from the lady with the cart and find out if I could read. I had my doubts. That evening, I lay down on my bed and held the book at the usual level for reading. I tried to read the first page of the novel, but, although my eyes saw the words, I couldn't decode their meanings. I didn't know whether the book was about a man and a woman, a school picnic, or any other subject. I couldn't concentrate long enough to get a general idea from that page of words, no matter how many times I "read" it. The fact that I could not read disturbed me, but my mind was still busy with so many confusing thoughts and with the remaining weird feelings in my head, that I didn't ponder the matter very long.

With my futile attempt at reading over, I walked out to the nurses' station in the hall outside my room. The mail that had arrived that afternoon was being distributed to the patients. I received two cards from Miami, one from Aunt Beth and the other from Aunt Louise, who'd also sent flowers. Aunt Louise wrote that in the next few days I would receive more cards.

Magazines were also being distributed. I noticed one with a beautiful woman on its cover that had a statement about how being very beautiful can sometimes cause problems. I wondered if that could be my problem, being pretty? That certainly was a different way of thinking about being good looking.

I decided that this hospital certainly was a lot different from what I'd imagined mental hospitals were like. All sorts of good things were happening to me there.

"There's a phone call for Elizabeth Martino," someone said.

"That's me. I'll take it." I walked over to the phone booth in the hall. "Hello."

"Liz, this is Mother. I'm glad you're all right. We were worried about you. How are you?"

"Oh, I'm fine, Mother," I replied. Why is she calling me? I wondered, while carrying on small talk with Mom. Is she going to continue with her attempts to kill me from Miami all the way up here in Iowa? I'll just talk to her for a minute or two longer and then we'll say our goodbyes. I was relieved to get off the phone and back to hospital life.

Bob Brown was a nice looking young man who was a fellow patient. His room was just down the hall from mine. We'd talked earlier that day and become friends. He came over to my room after I finished talking with Mom. I sat on my bed and looked at his handsome face in the dim evening light.

"I like good legs on a woman, Liz," he said to me, as we discussed what we liked about men and women.

"Since I've lost weight, I've got pretty good legs myself," I said to Bob, pulling my skirt up to my mid-thighs. I hoped he liked my legs. They'd always been so muscular from dancing and one of the heaviest parts of my body before I'd lost weight. I had lost fifteen lbs. during my pre-hospital illness.

"Not bad," Bob replied. Changing the subject, he asked me, "Did you know that I'm getting insulin treatments here?"

"No, I didn't know that," I replied. "What are they?"

"I don't know just how insulin shock works," he continued, "but they put me in a cold tub of water and shock me somehow."

"That sounds terrible, Bob. Doesn't the shock bother you?"

"I don't know," he replied. "I'm unconscious when they give it to me."

Two hours later, some men took Bob down the hall past the patients' rooms to another room, and gave him his treatment. At the time, I was taking a bath in a room nearby. I couldn't help wondering what insulin treatment was like, and if I'd ever be given that. But, it's not so bad here, I thought. I think Bob is the only patient who is getting those treatments.

My first few meals in the lunchroom at Blythe were a real treat. I didn't know why I responded so positively to eating with fellow patients. Maybe it was camaraderie with other "sufferers," "prisoners," or whatever they considered all of us to be. I only knew that I definitely reacted to the companionship at mealtime as though it was a "warm fuzzie." This feeling of companionship within my consciousness continued to grow. Different women in our section would get together in each other's rooms, drink coffee, and talk, and maybe work on some knitting that we had begun earlier in O.T.

The basic reason for the warmth I felt with these fellow women patients was the feeling that we all had something in common, that if one of us had to face the fact that she was insane, the rest of us were in the same predicament. We could face all of this together, helping each other. And, no one of us could look at another patient and laugh at her for being crazy, or be afraid of her. I had ascribed those kinds of opinions to people on the outside as I'd felt my sanity collapse.

On my fourth day in the better section, the thought came to my consciousness that most of the things I believed were happening weren't really happening at all. Rather, I had made them up; I had imagined them. I remembered that Dr. Cummings had implied just that. But that was not a pleasant thought. If that was true, then I would definitely have to face my insanity. I would have to change my self-concept from that of a woman endangered by threats from the outside, to one of an insane woman who was threatened not by outside forces, but by her own imagination and confusion. I wasn't sure that was the me I wanted to see, at least not yet.

Another one of the reasons I enjoyed my friends and my get-togethers with them was the actual attractiveness of our rooms in that section of the psychiatric wing. Each room had built-in dressers and closets, twin beds with chenille bedspreads, and private bathrooms. I also enjoyed the dayroom, which had a piano, television, and several chairs and sofas.

I was permitted to return to the first, or admitting ward, whenever I wanted. At one end of that ward there were Ping-Pong tables. I enjoyed several games with a couple of male attendants when I was in that section. There also were tables set up for card playing. Many evenings during my stay in Blythe, I played cards with other patients, mainly men. I remember feeling again the strange, prickly feelings in my head. It seemed as though my head was going to burst.

Although my strange thoughts were not as dominant by then, I still had some. I would watch television while I was the dummy in bridge, and I just knew that what the television personalities were saying had to do with me. There was a rather drastic change in my imaginative thinking, however, from a negative content to positive ones. I felt that, rather than being the target of murdering Communists, I was destined to go to Hollywood one day soon and become a famous dancer and movie star. These delusions were strengthened by the fact that I often danced in this same game room to music on the television after we finished our card games. One night I danced my way up to the office located between the two wards. The woman in the office watched me dance up the hall, and then kiddingly said, "I don't know, Elizabeth. Maybe I shouldn't let you back in this ward." She evidently wondered about my sanity.

It may have seemed to others I was doing very well. I definitely wasn't a problem patient, but I was still in my own dream world rather than the real world regardless of the impression I was making on others.

Sometime during my first week in Blythe, I began attending group therapy sessions every morning for about an hour and a half. The first couple weeks I was extremely quiet, saying, at the most, one or two words during the entire session. I was busy trying to decide just what this gathering of people represented. I looked at the different men and woman making up the group's circle. Soon I thought I'd figured out just where I was. Sure enough, I was in Heaven, and the other people in the group were also departed souls. Since I was in Heaven, I decided, I could probably find John Adams and John Quincy Adams.

I decided it would be a treat to find some of my ancestors. I surveyed the faces, trying to decide which persons were John Adams and his son. I never did find a face that looked like the pictures I'd seen of either famous man. As the days and weeks went by, I finally gave up my search. I concluded that the presence of the Adamses in this group was simply another figment of my overzealous imagination. Gradually I began to realize that, rather than the group of people being other-earthly, they simply were people who were searching for a better adjustment to life and the people in their lives.

Dr. Blackwell was our group leader. He was a psychologist. Aunt Phyllis had talked to him the day I was admitted to Blythe, and she later told me about their conversation. She'd told him what "good ancestry" I had, and about my "great potential." I wondered at the time what difference it made who and what my ancestors were, since I was a patient in a mental hospital. What good would it be to be a member of the D.A.R., if the local chapter was composed of loonies? At the time, I couldn't see how I could possibly ever accomplish anything comparable to the accomplishments of my ancestors, or for that matter, to those of my contemporary relatives. As far as I was concerned, I'd hit rock bottom, that is, if it was true that I was crazy. How much lower in status could I be since I was a nut in a "funny farm?"

I started traveling downtown twice a week to attend both a weekly group therapy session at Dr. Cummings' office, and an hourly session with a social worker. There was a clothing store at the bus stop where I waited for the bus to return from town to Blythe. It was one of the less expensive chain stores. These are the only kinds of clothes I'm going to be able to buy from now on, I would think, while waiting for my bus. I'll never be able to make enough money to buy nicer clothes, now that I'm so sick. I guess my status has really bottomed out.

Bob and I also took walks around Blythe. One time we walked all the way uptown and ate at a hotel restaurant. We didn't realize that we weren't supposed to walk that far from the hospital grounds. The next day, Dr. Blackwell very nicely told Bob and me that we shouldn't have gone so far, but he said he was sure that we hadn't been aware of the rule. After that, we confined our walks to around Blythe and the shopping center across the street.

I had paranoid feelings about the way people were thinking about me when I'd walk into the main lobby at Blythe. "I know those people think I'm strange, Dr. Blackwell," I told him one day after returning from a trip to the main lobby.

"I'm sure they aren't thinking that, Liz" he replied. "You have a very special look about you. You're an attractive woman. I'm sure that's all they were thinking."

I wasn't convinced that Dr. Blackwell was right.

****

216

"When I get out of here, I'm going to slit my wrist!" A friend said this several times to me in the lunchroom, speaking with a determined voice.

Can she really mean that? I wondered. Why would anyone want to die, actually want to end her life?

"You can't mean that, Rhonda," I told her one day.

"Oh, yes I do. What is there for me to live for, anyway? Men have treated me like shit ever since I was a child. I was raped when I was ten, again when I was twelve, and where have I ended up now? In the funny farm! I have nothing to live for."

Is this where we mental patients end up? I wondered. Do we get so depressed about our condition and bad luck that we don't even want to live? I sincerely hope I don't end up feeling that way.

The next day I mentioned Rhonda's conversation to Dr. Cummings. "Liz, I want you to start associating with normal, mentally healthy people," he told me, "not just other patients. It's not good for you to interact only with psychiatric patients."

"But, I feel close to my friends here, Dr. Cummings. We have so much in common, and I don't feel threatened by them."

"Still, please take my advice, Liz," he reiterated. "Why don't you start spending your weekends with your family? I'll be happy to approve weekend passes. That would be good therapy for you."

"All right. That's fine with me," I answered.

I soon found that, although I did enjoy weekends, I came back to Blythe exhausted. It took me until Tuesday or Wednesday of each week to rest up from my weekends.

I was in Blythe for one month. After that, Dr. Cummings decided I was ready to go home. We made plans for my discharge. The day I left Blythe, I was waiting in the dayroom for Aunt Phyllis to come for me. All of a sudden, as I stood there watching television, I realized for the first time that that people on TV were simply actors and actresses acting out their parts, that they were not trying to relay some secret message to me. They didn't even realize I existed there at Blythe Hospital in Iowa. I finally realized that all my strange thoughts were figments of my imagination, that I was, indeed, mentally ill. What a psychological blow. I was actually crazy. Crazy. These imaginative thoughts I was having represented what is referred to as insanity.

Oh, no! I thought. This is terrible. How can I live with this? How can I ever face myself again, knowing I'm insane? I began to develop a terrible headache.

Soon Aunt Phyllis and Kenny arrived and took me home. I had learned just that day that my diagnosis was "Paranoid Schizophrenia." That's what Dr. Cummings told me when I asked him. That was also a blow to my mind, and I wondered, will I ever be able to function normally at home or anywhere now that I know the truth about myself?

Chapter Twelve

I'D RATHER BE DEAD

Des Moines/Miami 1963

A unt Phyllis and Uncle Gerald offered to let Kenny and me live with them while I completed my recovery. While in Blythe, I had hoped to be able to move into an apartment of my own for Kenny and me. But I decided to take them up on their offer and moved back in. They had such a beautiful home, and I loved their whole family. Perhaps this would be my haven.

Soon things became rather routine for me. Three days a week I worked at Uncle Gerald's nursing home, and the other four days I worked around the house and took care of Kenny. Aunt Phyllis turned part of their basement into a suite for us. She even bought us a beautiful hanging chandelier. I was pleased with Kenny's and my basement apartment.

Kenny was a very happy child. He was in a good environment and much loved by the Duncan family. He had many friends in the neighborhood who would come by for him each morning and take him outside to play. Winter soon passed, and spring brought nice weather for their games and sports. Kenny became very popular with the neighborhood children, and this alleviated my problems with having to entertain him.

I enjoyed working in the nursing home, where Mrs. Keller was my supervisor. We worked with some of the residents, helping them with various arts and crafts, taking them for walks and providing other activities. The nursing home was a very old building. Most of the residents were also quite elderly, and they enjoyed our efforts to make their time pass more pleasantly. I found this work rewarding.

Evenings after I'd returned from work, Aunt Phyllis would have dinner ready, and then she would tell me to relax. She insisted she would do the dishes saying, "After all, today you were a working girl."

Aunt Phyllis had a maid six mornings a week, from 7 a.m. to 1 p.m. They kept an immaculate house, even though the home was quite large. She worked right along with the maid, and I helped on the days I was home. I cleaned the main bathroom and thought I wasn't cleaning dirt, that I was simply cleaning basins and tiles that were already clean. The house never had a chance to get dirty.

Aunt Phyllis and Uncle Gerald's family attended the local Congregational Church. Every Sunday morning, we all went to church. I began considering having Kenny baptized there. I realized that my crude attempt to baptize him in Miami wasn't an actual or official baptism. So, one Sunday morning, I carried Kenny down front to the minister, where he sprinkled Kenny's forehead. Afterwards, tears wet my face, as I believed Kenny had been blessed.

It wasn't long, however, before I became quite bored at home. My main problem, however, was a serious depression. I was mainly depressed about the fact that I was a mental patient, that I had actually experienced insanity and now had to live with that realization. I continued with group therapy once a week with Dr. Cummings, and I also attended an hourly weekly session with my social worker. Dr. Cummings' explanation for my depression was that it represented an outpouring of repressed feelings buried since my childhood. These were feelings which I had not been able to experience at the time of the trauma. I had repressed my emotions, and they were now coming into consciousness because I was in a good environment with Aunt Phyllis and Uncle Gerald. He prescribed Elavil, an antidepressant. But my depression remained, and it seemed to worsen, until I, like Rhonda, wanted to die. I was constantly aware that I'd experienced madness, and I felt that I was not coping with life as my family thought I should, that I was letting them down. I became convinced that I would be happier with God, wherever He was. I didn't believe I could ever be happy here on earth.

My Baptist faith had taught me that if we're once saved, we're always saved, so I didn't think God would send me to Hell if I took my life. I felt that I didn't have much to live for. One Sunday while eating lunch at the club with Uncle Gerald and his family I spoke out saying, "I wish I was dead!" I thought that someone would get mad at me, but no one did. This was a cry for help.

I had other problems as well. One day I stood in the back yard with Kenny playing nearby, and thought, how can I cope with everything I have to deal with now? Mom raised me, without me knowing my father.

Now I had to raise my son alone without my husband. Not only did I have to bear the burden of being a child without a father, now I also had to bear the burden of being a mother alone. I really didn't know if I could cope with my life under those circumstances. Another problem was that the new medicine, Elavil, didn't agree with me. I asked Dr. Cummings to take me off it, and he did. As the weeks went by, I thought more often about suicide. However, I was aware that if I attempted to take my life and failed, my aunt and uncle would probably never forgive me, and my life would be worse rather that better. For this reason, I decided not to attempt suicide in Des Moines.

Shortly after arriving home from Blythe, I wanted to return there. I was finding it hard to cope at home, even while participating in the simplest activities. After a couple of weeks, Aunt Phyllis agreed to let me go back to the hospital. I think she felt that if I wanted to be there so badly, I might as well go back and get my dependency feelings for the hospital out of my system.

I was in Blythe the second time for only one week. While there, I was romanced by an older man, who seemed taken with me and talked about taking me to

Europe with him. His plans fell through, however, when Uncle Gerald got wind of his scheme. He knew this man had a shady reputation. He felt the man had ulterior motives, such as Uncle Gerald's wealth, that his attraction to me wasn't love. While our romance lasted, it temporarily lifted my spirits, but soon I found myself back home with Uncle Gerald's family.

That summer, my fifteen-year-old cousin Betty decided to take a speed-reading course at her high school. Aunt Phyllis and I agreed it would be nice for me to take the course with her. Poor Betty. I probably seemed like a drab companion for her that summer, and I did terribly in the course. When I was a teenager, I had easily received nearly all A's. Now I couldn't even keep up with students five years younger than I. I started in the middle group, speed-wise. Before long I was put down with the slow group, and finally I was doing so poorly and was so discouraged that I quit the course altogether. I could read, but I couldn't speed read as well as high school juniors. Once more, I had failed.

During those days in Iowa, I often thought that if I could have private psychotherapy with Dr. Cummings twice a week, I could improve. Every time I spoke to him about it, he asked me whether I thought I could have a better relationship with a male or a female therapist. When I told him I'd rather see a man, he suggested that, in that case, I shouldn't see him, but rather my social worker, who was a woman. He said I evidently needed to improve my relationships with women. I told him I didn't feel that I got much out of my sessions with my social worker, although she was a very nice person. I believed I could benefit more from him as a private therapist. I really liked him, because he was kind and understanding. I felt that talking more with him, in an effort to rebuild my life, would be beneficial.

He agreed to see me for psychotherapy, but when I spoke to Aunt Phyllis about the possibility of Uncle Gerald helping me pay for the therapy, she replied, "People just can't go to a psychiatrist for every little problem in life, Liz. I don't run to a psychiatrist with every little problem of mine. You're already receiving sufficient therapy, and besides, what you have in mind would be awfully expensive."

So, that hope was gone. Life was even drearier than before. I knew I'd been insane. I was living with severe depression, and there was no way out. I didn't think I could rebuild my personality alone. I began to wish I could go into a state hospital and not be released until I was cured. I knew that Rhonda had been in a state hospital after leaving Blythe, and she had found her stay there helpful. I thought that care at a state hospital would be even more thorough than at a smaller hospital.

Aunt Phyllis thought this idea strange, but I continued to daydream about it. In my mind, I pictured a brick building with a high fence around it. In this sanctuary, I dreamed, I would work to cover my expenses, while dedicated psychiatrists strove to help me rebuild my sanity and mental health. I didn't know if I could ever work things out so this dream would come true, but I held on to the dream.

By then, I was getting along much better with Mom. I talked to her several times on the phone, and each time I felt so much warmth from her that it made me want to be with her. I had realized, since the day I left Blythe the first time, that Mom had my best interests at heart, that she never wanted me dead. Mom was so understanding. After all, she was the only relative this side of the Mississippi who had lived with me through my private hell with Carl. No one else understood the entire mental trauma I had received while living with him those thirteen years.

Instead of feeling fear of Mom, I began to feel that being around her would be beneficial to my security and well-being. I wished I was back in Miami. I also felt a pull towards Miami, as though there might be help for me there. Maybe the doctor I needed was there.

For the most part, it had been Uncle Gerald and Aunt Phyllis's contention that I should not be with Mom, that she had been the main person responsible for my breakdown. They had not had the misfortune of knowing Carl Jones well. They did not realize that it was his negative influence which had caused such damage to my ego and stability. Instead, they blamed Mother. However, gradually, my aunt and uncle approved my return to Miami. Although they never said anything to me, I felt that I was quite a burden to them due to all of my problems and the expenses of both Kenny and me.

I decided that I would like to have Kenny stay in Des Moines for a few more months, because I felt I needed a chance to get back on my feet, and then I could resume caring for him. At first, Aunt Phyllis didn't like this idea. She did, however, finally agree to my plan for her to care for Kenny until the following Christmas. I knew that I would have to be the one to tell Kenny I was leaving. He was just two years old, but I felt he would at least understand some of what I would tell him. A couple of days before I left Des Moines, I spoke to Kenny while dressing him. "Kenny, Mommy's going back to Miami. I'm sick and I need some time to get well. When I'm better, I'll come back for you, I hope by Christmas. I promise I'll be back; don't forget that I love you very much."

He didn't say anything. What does a two-year-old say to such a proclamation? But I believed he understood more than was obvious. After talking with Kenny about leaving, I remembered all the times he would come running out to greet me home from work, happily running toward me, a big smile on his face, yelling, "Mommy's home! Mommy's home!"

When I got back to Miami, I stayed with Mom in a small, one-bed room apartment in Coconut Grove, just three or four blocks from Aunt Beth and Uncle Joseph's home.

I knew I still needed to see a psychiatrist, so I went to the Jackson Memorial Hospital Psychiatric

Clinic and was placed on their waiting list. I could not psychologically afford to go without psychiatric care while awaiting an appointment at Jackson Clinic. I began seeing a private psychiatrist for weekly, half-hour sessions. I finally had a doctor for psychotherapy. I feared however, that half-hour sessions would be inadequate for my needs. Yet, it would be hard enough to afford even that much of the doctor's time.

"My name is Dr. Garson, Elizabeth. I understand you were recently in a private psychiatric hospital in Iowa."

"Yes, I was," I replied. "I hope that now I can get well. I've left my two-year-old son with my aunt and uncle up north, but I miss him so much. I hope it won't be too long before I'll be able to have him back with me."

"Elizabeth, your situation is similar to a woman who is recovering from a fractured leg or hip. We wouldn't ask her to get busy and do lots of house-work until she recovered, and we shouldn't ask you to handle all of your responsibilities until you've recovered." Dr. Garson was certainly very pleasant. He was rather young, wore glasses, and had a warm personality.

When the session was over, Mom and I went to get a cup of coffee at a drug store nearby. I sat next to a middle-aged man who soon began talking to me. "Do you work around here?" he asked. As he spoke, I noticed he seemed different from most people. I wasn't quite sure why he was unusual, but something was out of the ordinary.

"No, I'm not working right now," I replied. "I've just been to see my doctor."

"What kind of doctor?" he asked.

"A psychiatrist," I said, rather irked by his boldness.

"Oh, one of those shrinks. I used to see one of them myself, but since my operation I haven't had to see one much."

"Operation!" I said, surprised. "What kind of operation did you have?"

"A lobotomy. Haven't you heard of them? A few years ago psychiatrists were doing lobotomies right and left."

So, that's what's unusual about this man, I thought. They've done something surgically inside his head and it's affected the way he acts. Boy, I'm sure glad I didn't have to have brain surgery.

After finishing our coffee, Mom and I returned to our small apartment, my haven. But it wasn't much of a haven for me. Mom worked long hours, five days a week. I stayed around home reading, talking to the lady next door, and occasionally going with her to the beach. Every morning when Mom left, I would cry and tell her that I didn't know if I could make it through the day alone. I could see from her response that she was concerned, but we both knew she had to work to support us.

One morning, as I wept uncontrollably, she hugged me and said, "Liz, you've got your whole life ahead of you. There are many good things in store for you. You have a lot to your advantage. You're young, beautiful, and intelligent."

I thought, for having so many good attributes, I sure do feel terribly depressed. I don't see myself in the same light that Mom sees me.

Carolyn Price, the girl who had noticed symptoms of emotional illness within herself that year at Trinity Bible College, had been in a state psychiatric hospital for a year after leaving Trinity. She had written me several times over the years. She had recovered after her stay in the hospital, gone back to college, and recently graduated. She felt fantastic about life. Each spring she sent me her class picture. When I got especially depressed, I looked at Carolyn's latest picture. If she can get well and look so good, I would think, maybe I can, too, someday. Maybe there is hope for me.

The main pictures I looked at during those days, however, were those of Kenny. I cried, feeling guilty for leaving him in Iowa and wishing he was with me. I must not be much of a mother, I thought, if I can leave my own son in one state and go to another state, thousands of miles away. I'm just a failure. I can't even succeed at something as basic as being a mother to my son. Carl must have been right. I must be no good.

I was bored, along with being depressed. I decided to find a part-time job. There was a department store in downtown Miami that hired sales people to work 5:30 to 9:30 in the evenings and all day on Saturdays. I went for an interview, and soon was taking the bus back and forth to a sales job in Ladies' Dresses.

Working didn't ease my mental pain much, however, since my department wasn't busy and I was left with lots of time to think. Thinking wasn't my most successful endeavor at that point. Many nights, after returning home from work, I would lie in bed after taking the prescribed sleeping pill I had taken ever since my stay in Blythe. As I lay there, my thoughts tormented me. I'm insane, I'm actually insane, I would think, feeling there was no relief to be found for me. I don't have to worry anymore that maybe one day I'll "go off the deep end." I already have. It wasn't a pleasant way to fall asleep.

I thought about suicide again. Now that I was with Mom, I knew she loved me unconditionally. She wouldn't hate me forever if I attempted to take my life and ended up failing. Soon, I thought, Uncle Gerald will be sending me a new supply of sleeping capsules. I can always swallow some. I decided that sleeping pills were an effective method for my self-destruction. I don't have anything to live for, anyway, I decided. I wish someone would just help me organize my life and my personality again. But there seems to be no hope for that. There's no use for me to stay around here on earth with my head in the state it's in.

A couple of days later I received the bottle of 100 sleeping capsules. I planned how to leave my gross earthly problems behind me. I would wait for Mom to go to work and then simply take lots of capsules. Mom left for work on my selected morning, not suspecting anything. Around noon, I finally got up enough courage to swallow the capsules. I poured myself a tall glass of water, opened the bottle and began swallowing and counting. "One pill down, two, three, four ... fifty-six, fifty-seven, fifty-eight ... seventy-four, seventy-five, seventy-six, seventy-seven."

My head was swimming. I can't hold the glass any more, I thought. I'd better stop; I must have taken enough. What will I do? I know, I'll walk to the park right now.

When I walked out and shut the door of our apartment, I didn't lock it. Somehow, I managed to stumble the three blocks to the park. That's where I ended up, lying on the grass in Coconut Grove Park.

The next feelings I experienced were bliss, peace, and happiness. I felt as though I was near God or with Him. I thought that maybe I was so near death that He was close by, waiting for me to join Him or return to the living, depending upon the expertise and skill of my doctors. I was certain that God is goodness itself, and I was not afraid to die.

Who is that blue person walking next to me? Where am I? I opened my eyes slightly, and caught a glimpse of a girl in a blue uniform, walking next to my bed. Soon I was back deep in sleep and in peace with God. The sequence repeated itself until I finally opened my eyes enough to stay awake.

The blissful feelings, the good part, fled when I was fully awake. I felt miserable, more miserable than ever. Oh, no, I thought. I don't want to wake up if it means feeling these same old depressed feelings. Why couldn't I have stayed where I was peaceful with God? I wish I hadn't awakened.

"Liz! Thank God you're alive!" Mom stood next to my bed, a big smile covering her face. "God's answered my prayers! You've had three doctors working to save your life for a day and a half. They had the nurses take your blood pressure every fifteen minutes."

"Where am I, Mom?" I asked, dazed and unsure.

"You're in the hospital, in the neurology section," Mom replied, lovingly. "The doctors were afraid they might have to do a tracheotomy, but fortunately, they didn't have to. I'm so thrilled and relieved that you're back with us. I'm also glad that a man found you in the park and called an ambulance. Thank God for that man."

"I guess I'm glad also, but I feel so terrible. All my awful depressed feelings are back."

One afternoon, some young adults visited my roommate. I could hear one young man say, "Do you know Jesus Christ as your Lord and Savior? We'd like to explain to you how to become a born-again Christian."

I didn't hear what my roommate said in reply, but I knew I didn't want to speak to those Christians. Talking that way disturbed me. I was disappointed in God. Even though I knew Jesus was still my Lord and Savior, I couldn't understand why I had gone crazy when I was trying my hardest to be a good Christian. To my relief, the Christian witnesses left without coming to talk to me.

I was in the medical section of Jackson Hospital for two weeks. Several doctors talked to me about my mental state. One doctor, Dr. Ahmed, told me he had seen me when the ambulance brought me to Jackson. He had requested that I be transferred to Neurology. He was the chief resident, in charge of Neurology. Dr. Ahmed made a special trip to talk to me one afternoon about my love life.

"Liz, do you have many friends?" Dr. Ahmed looked at me intently.

"Well, I've just returned from Iowa. I don't really have too many friends here yet. But I'll probably make some soon."

"Okay. How about men? Do you have boy friends?"

I thought Dr. Ahmed was trying to find out if I was normal sexually.

"You were married once, right?"

"Yes, briefly."

"Did you and your husband get along all right, sex-wise?"

"Yes. Our sex life was fine. I got pregnant on our honeymoon."

"How about when you were younger?" he continued. "Did you have good relationships with boys?"

"Sure, I dated a lot."

"Were you ever disgusted with sex, or did you enjoy it and your relationship with men?"

"I've always enjoyed sex. In fact, I think it's great!"

" Good, Liz. You seem pretty normal to me."

"Well, maybe I'm normal sexually," I said. "But I sure don't feel normal otherwise."

****

Soon I was able to walk down to the dayroom and watch TV. Physically, I had a rough time trying to get my strength back. I had stressed my body with the sleeping capsules. During my stay in Neurology, they took me off psychiatric medication because of all the sleeping pills already in my system.

Dr. Ahmed told me I had the choice of either going home or being admitted to the psychiatric wing as an in-patient. He said it was up to me. I opted for becoming a psychiatric patient. I realized I had to do something to get well, or at least improve. Otherwise, I'd probably pull a repeat performance of my suicide attempt.

One evening, as I sat in the dayroom in front of the TV, not paying attention to it, Dr. Garson stopped by to see me. His voice was warm. "How are you, Elizabeth?"

"Not well. I feel terrible. I'm all set to go to the psychiatric wing, but it probably won't help. Probably nothing will. I don't think I'll ever get well."

"I think you will, Elizabeth. I have faith in you and in your ability to recover." Dr. Garson smiled, said goodbye and walked on. I thought he was awfully nice to encourage me. I didn't agree with his prognosis, but a little feeling of hope rose within me.

I thought, for all I know, I might even be assigned to a great doctor in the psychiatric wing, the magic one who will help me restructure my life and personality. Maybe I can be rehabilitated.

Chapter Thirteen

DR. GOLDBERG, PSYCHIATRIST AND FRIEND

Miami, 1963

J ackson Memorial Hospital Psychiatric Wing, called the Institute, lacked Blythe Psychiatric Ward's fancy trimmings. I shared a room with three other women, and we had a joint small chest of drawers and a small closet. Wondering what this admission would bring, I walked into the dayroom, sat down and watched television.

"Elizabeth Martino." A middle-aged man, with a pipe in his hand and a twinkle in his eye had entered the dayroom, obviously looking for me.

"I'm Liz," I said, walking up to him.

"Liz, I'm Dr. Goldberg." I couldn't help noticing my new doctor's friendliness. He looked very kind, reminding me of my grandoo. Already my hopes were up.

"I'll probably be seeing you often. Let's go to my office now and talk about our plans for your therapy."

I followed Dr. Goldberg to his office, and there he proceeded to evaluate me. He completed a report on his findings, which he submitted to his superior, who was a psychoanalyst. Dr. Goldberg told me he'd been a general practitioner on Miami Beach for several years, and that he'd recently begun his residency in psychiatry at the University of Miami at Jackson Memorial Hospital.

Dr. Goldberg said that he could tell from our first session that he and I would have lots to talk about. He said he would see me six hours a week for private psychotherapy in the beginning, and twice a week for group therapy sessions with him and another resident psychiatrist.

With our first session completed, we walked back to my ward. Dr. Goldberg took a small key from his pocket and unlocked the door to let me back into the dayroom. He looked at me as he unlocked the door, and again I saw the twinkle in his eyes and a big smile on his face. He said reassuringly, "I believe things will go well, Liz. Take care, I'll see you tomorrow." I knew then that my sessions with Dr. Philip Goldberg would be the happiest parts of my days at the Institute.

As our sessions progressed, I told Mother one evening that, although I felt miserable most days, Dr. Goldberg's help was so wonderful. "When I see him for therapy sessions, I feel as though good things are happening to me. I believe that with him there is hope."

In one of our sessions, I asked Dr. Goldberg how he was able to spend so much time seeing me. His response was that President Kennedy had increased funding for the care of mental health patients, which resulted in his having only fifteen patients. He had selected three of the most promising young adults to focus on. I was one of the three, and that was why he had so much time for me. This made me very happy, and I thanked him and felt blesses by President Kennedy.

Dr. Goldberg and I talked for hours and hours about my early years, my family, my stepfather, and everything about me. I also told him about my recent illness and hospitalizations. He listened attentively, and I could see in his facial expressions that he cared about my mental and emotional recovery.

"I can't see that much wrong with you, Liz," Dr. Goldberg said to me one day. "That is, except for the fact that you've told me how you were out of touch with reality for a while, but those delusions only lasted for a couple of months. I think that if you were to be evaluated by a board of psychiatrists right now, they would all agree there is nothing wrong with you."

"That may be true," I said, "but I sure don't feel normal. When I leave here each day and go back to the ward, I feel miserable until the next time I get to see you. Can't you give me some sort of medicine to make me feel better?"

"Right now I want you off your medicine, Liz," he answered. "You will feel your feelings more authentically without being medicated, and that will help us do a better job with your psychotherapy. This way you will know and understand how you really feel about your life and the people in it. However, I will prescribe some Melaril for you to take occasionally if you start feeling especially bad or depressed."

"Good," I said, relieved. At least maybe I could depend on taking something for relief once in a while.

Often, when I returned to the ward following therapy, I'd tell my fellow patients some of the things I learned from Dr. Goldberg. A couple of friends told me that they thought I'd make a good psychiatrist myself, that they'd like to have me for their doctor.

Dr. Goldberg told me that during my developmental years I had not formed a healthy self-concept. He told me how important self-esteem is in life and how tragic a person's life can become if they have a "poor opinion" of themselves. The understanding of this terribly important aspect of personality helped me restructure my thinking, as did many of Dr. Goldberg's other helpful teachings.

Dr. Goldberg told me my friends in Kenniltown probably liked me more than I realized. He informed me that I might have been projecting my negative self-image onto what my friends thought of me. It was not my friends who thought I was "no good," rather it was my negative projection.

I remember telling Dr. Goldberg one day about the parties we had in Kenniltown when I was seven. "We played spin the bottle, but I used to feel so bad because somehow I never would get selected. I never got to kiss the boys in the closet."

"Liz, they didn't know what they were missing!"

When he said that to me, it felt so good. He evidently found me attractive and that I must have been a pretty little girl, and not undesirable.

Although Dr. Goldberg behaved in a fatherly way toward me, I couldn't help admiring that wonderful man. He was a great doctor, and he was also a good friend. Although he considered me as his patient, and someone he showed great concern for, I began to find myself becoming attracted to him. Dr. Goldberg was older than I and married, but I sure did feel as though I loved him more than I'd ever loved any man. However, I knew he was just my doctor.

Dr. Goldberg also stated that I had been passive in expressing my emotions when it came to dealing with Carl. He told me he that knew a lot of children who would have told such a man to "go jump off a cliff," or "go out and play in traffic," if that man had treated them the way Carl treated me. He didn't understand my response of turning the other cheek rather than fighting back. That confused me.

Although Dr. Goldberg boosted me from my state of desperation, I still felt miserable most of the time, particularly when away from him. A black cloud settled over my head and permeated to my brain, creating havoc and destruction, and rendering me unable to fully function as a human being. I felt depressed, miserable, and life did not seem very desirable.

I did make a good friend, however, whose name was Jane. She was also diagnosed with schizophrenia, and could recount, as I could, imaginary thoughts from her most severe illness. We shared our mutual concern of recovering.

"One day I'm going to write a book about my experiences, Jane," I told her one afternoon as we walked around the Institute grounds.

"Everyone who has a breakdown says that, Liz," she replied.

"Maybe you'll write about it; maybe you won't."

"Have you ever been married, Jane?" I asked, changing the subject.

"Yes, and I have three children. They're with my ex-husband. He got custody of them because of my illness." Jane looked sad. I thought to myself that she must miss her children terribly, as I missed Kenny.

A couple of days later, I walked around the ward just after I washed my hair. Dr. Goldberg and some other people I'd never met, walked up to me.

"This is Liz Martino," he told them.

"Liz, this is Mrs. Greenhill and Mr. Eckbert. They're interested in meeting you and learning about your case."

What a time to bring people around to meet me, I thought. My hair's still wet, and I feel especially depressed today. They're bound to think I'm in a terrible state.

"There's not much wrong with Mrs. Martino," Dr. Goldberg continued. "She's really quite mentally healthy."

"That might be what you think, Dr. Goldberg," I said. "But I feel terrible."

Dr. Goldberg didn't seem disturbed by the comments I made in front of his associates. They talked for a few minutes more and left the ward.

That evening Mom and Aunt Beth came to visit me, as they often did. This particular visit distressed me. Why are they sitting there with those expressions on their faces? I thought, as I sat curled up on the day-room couch in front of the TV. I didn't talk to them because I was convinced they didn't love me. In fact, I believed they didn't even like me. Not talking to them will serve them right for feeling that way about me, I decided.

For their part, my aunt and mother spoke to each other and to some of the other patients and seemed unconcerned about my behavior. After a while, they kissed me goodbye and left for home.

Oh, so they think a kiss will make everything all right? I thought. Well, it won't! I can't wait until I see Dr. Goldberg tomorrow. I'm so depressed now. I can't wait until our session.

The following morning, I dressed, put my makeup on meticulously, as always, walked up the corridor, took the elevator to the second floor, and walked down the hall to Dr. Goldberg's office.

"Dr. Goldberg, do I ever have bad news to tell you! Last night my mother and Aunt Beth both visited me, and I learned something from the visit. I discovered that they hate me."

"Liz, what proof do you have for such an accusation?" Dr. Goldberg stayed calm. He didn't seem upset about what I'd told him.

"Proof?" I asked astounded. "I guess my proof is the expressions they had on their faces."

"That doesn't sound like very conclusive proof to me, Liz. If they'd come right out and said they didn't like you, that might be proof." Dr. Goldberg smiled as he spoke.

"Liz," he continued, "I want you to start a mental process right now that I call 'testing reality.' That means that every time you're tempted to think paranoid-type thoughts such as the ones you had last night, you should purposely stop yourself, unless you have definite proof."

"I don't know if I can do that, Dr. Goldberg. That sounds awfully hard. I'll give it a try, though." As I considered applying this new principle, I didn't know if I'd have the strength and will to no longer ascribe negative motives to others. Though difficult in the beginning, the process paid off and was very rewarding. I used "reality testing" to deter myself from thinking paranoid thoughts.

Dr. Goldberg felt I also needed to broaden my horizons as part of my therapy. He suggested I read the daily paper. Shortly thereafter, I found myself sitting on the lawn in front of the Institute, reading the newspaper from beginning to end. Unfortunately, I found it to be a chore, rather than something enjoyable. In fact, a great distance separated my world of depression from the real world where everyone else lived. I felt so separated from the real world that on the day of President Kennedy's assassination, I had trouble grieving the world's great loss. I sat and watched the President's funeral and found, rather than crying over his death, I kept worrying about my own personal problems. The gap widened between worlds.

I stayed in the Institute for three months. Before I left, Dr. Goldberg put me on a low dose of Trilafon, a medication similar to the Stelazine I'd taken in Iowa and upon my return to Florida. Amazed at how much better I looked after beginning the Trilafon, Dr. Goldberg commented that my posture had improved. I felt better, so much so, that I felt well enough to try going home. The next problem was where would I live? Dr. Goldberg, my relatives and I agreed that living with Mom again would not be best, since she was gone during the day. I remembered Aunt Beth and Uncle Joseph's offer to stay with them. I told Dr. Goldberg I'd like to live there, if they would still have me. He called them, and they came in for a conference with him and me. Soon, things were all set for me to go home. Once again, I would be back in Coconut

Grove with my family. Maybe this time things would go better.

Chapter Fourteen

RELAPSE

Miami, 1964

T hings did go better, at first. My personality was in the process of being restructured, with the help of my good doctor. His reality-testing technique was beginning to reap benefits, and I felt there was hope for my mental health and me. I felt better.

I was back in the beautiful country-style home on Greenwood Road. It was late fall, and it rained quite a bit. Aunt Beth and Uncle Joseph gave me a beautiful raincoat and umbrella set for my birthday. I enjoyed walking through the Grove in my new outfit. Things were looking up. I even attracted a young male artist one day while walking along in my new finery. He told me that when he saw me, he thought I had "real class." We had a couple of dates. Unfortunately, I told him about my recent illness. He told me I was the kind of girl he really liked, but he never called me again. I was tempted to worry that he was afraid of my craziness, but I promptly utilized my new technique to fight paranoia.

I was still seeing Father. My stepmother was not aware of our meetings. She was concerned about Mother's motives. Father and I would often go out to lunch. I was beginning to be very pleased by his attention. He was warm and easy to get along with. The experiences came across as "warm fuzzies."

The main problem bothering me was Kenny's absence. I wanted him back with me, and I kept telling that to Dr. Goldberg. I was still seeing him twice a week for individual therapy and group therapy once a week.

"Hi, Dr. Cantor, how are you?" I spoke to Dr. Goldberg's associate as I entered the room for group therapy one morning.

"I'm fine, thanks, Liz. How are you doing now that you're home from the hospital?"

"Oh, good," I replied. "I feel so much better now that I'm taking Trilafon. Just how do those medicines work, Dr. Cantor—do you know?"

"You know, Liz," he answered, "We really don't know that. All that's known about the medicines is that they seem to control psychiatric conditions somehow."

Control, I thought. I'm glad at least they do that. Trilafon must be doing some sort of controlling for me. Thank God, I'm no longer simply "miserating," a word I'd come up with to describe my depressed feelings.

Dr. Goldberg came into the room. I looked at him and immediately felt my warm feelings toward him, my combination of fatherly-love and romantic attraction. Group was good, as always, though I did not enjoy it as much as Dr. Goldberg's and my individual sessions. I liked having more attention. I liked having more of a chance to work on solving my own thought-distortion problems.

Group therapy gave me opportunities to learn how to relate better to my peers, which was also very beneficial. We tried to help each other cope, and in doing so we learned how to get along better with other people.

A week or so later at an individual session, I again questioned Dr. Goldberg, "When can I go get

Kenny?" Dr. Goldberg had heard me ask this question often, but this time he seemed more responsive.

"Well, Liz, if you think you're ready to cope with having a small child around to care for, it's fine with me for you to take the trip up north and bring him back. I find you're doing much better now."

"Oh, thank you, thank you, Dr. Goldberg. You're wonderful! I'll start planning for the trip today."

As our session continued, I had other questions. "You know, Dr. Goldberg, people certainly do seem to have their prejudices regarding mental illness, don't they? I was dating a young man who seemed to be crazy about me at first, but when I told him about my condition, he seemed to back off and I haven't heard from him since."

"Yes, Liz, there is a lot of prejudice. I believe that it's due to a person's fear of losing his own sanity, sort of a defensive and protective response on his part."

"Probably some of the scariest aspects of mental illness, or at least of schizophrenia," I continued, "are all the imaginary thoughts that make up the sick person's delusions."

"You know, Liz," Dr. Goldberg commented, "Those imaginary thoughts are very much the same as the dreams we all have at night while we are asleep. The psychotic person is simply dreaming in the daytime."

"Really?" I asked in surprise. "How do you mean dreaming? Normal people only dream during their sleep."

"When a person is psychotic that simply means that his ego is not functioning adequately," he went on. "In psychiatry, the ego is a person's reality tester, not his vanity. When we sleep our egos are not keeping us in touch with the realities of our environment as they normally do during our waking state. Therefore, our unconscious, or id, breaks through to consciousness and we have our fantasies, or dreams. An insane person is simply experiencing this same state while awake, because the stresses and pressures of his life have broken down his ego and its ability to keep his id under control."

"Wow!" I said enthusiastically. "Then that doesn't make me such a 'weirdo,' after all, because I had some imaginary thoughts during my illness. Everybody dreams. I was just dreaming more of the time than most people."

"Yes, I believe other people fear they will not always be able to keep a lid on their own unconscious, or id. They feel threatened to know that this has happened to someone else, so it could happen to them, hence their prejudice. They may not have insight or understanding as to the basis of their prejudice, but this may be the root cause."

Dr. Goldberg's statements made sense. I was excited and relieved by his simple explanation for insanity, that it's just another form of dreaming. I no longer felt set apart from the rest of humanity because of what I'd experienced.

A week or so later, I prepared for my trip to Iowa to reunite with Kenny. At least I don't have to pack any sleeping pills, I thought, while packing my bag. Dr. Goldberg had stopped my reliance on pills for sleep. It was a good thing, too, because if I ever became suicidal again, the pills would be much too effective a method for killing myself.

I thought back to the nights in Jackson when Dr. Goldberg made me stop relying on pills for falling asleep. He told me that he didn't need anything for sleeping, so I shouldn't either. He wanted me to wait until I fell asleep. I was getting enough rest and leisure time in the hospital to afford a little sleepless time at night, if necessary, he told me. I needed to relearn the art of falling asleep naturally. He said that if I stayed awake until 3:00 or 4:00 a.m. I could ask for something, but otherwise I should try not taking anything. He said that before long I would be able to fall asleep more easily. It worked. I only had to ask for a sleeping pill the first two nights. From then on I fell asleep without any medical assistance.

****

I arrived in Des Moines in the middle of a cold December night, 1963. Aunt Phyllis met me at the train station and we drove off to her home in the suburbs. To my surprise, when I walked down the stairs to the basement, I saw Kenny, wide awake, standing in his crib.

"Hi, Mommy!" He called out to me, jumping up and down on his crib.

"Hi, Honey," I replied, picking him up in my arms. It was so good to see Kenny, but I wondered why he was still up. Had he been expecting me? Aunt Phyllis said that she told him his mommy was coming to get him that night and take him home with her. He must have understood Aunt Phyllis and cared enough to stay awake awaiting my arrival. I was thrilled that Kenny had cared that much. Aunt Phyllis also told me that she had Kenny calling her and Uncle Gerald "Mommy" and "Daddy," since they were his present parent-figures. Even so, he'd remembered me well enough as his real Mommy to wait up for me until one o'clock in the morning. I was impressed.

My aunt and uncle were delighted to see how well I was doing. They were very interested to hear about my doctor's care and the various teachings and techniques he was using, especially intensive psychotherapy. I went to see Dr. Cummings and my former social worker while in town, and they were also impressed with my improved health.

Uncle Gerald mentioned one day that he hoped the next time we saw each other I would be driving. That concerned me, because I had problems whenever I thought about driving. I had fearful visions about my driving so recklessly that I would purposefully drive off a bridge, or something else, in a suicide attempt.

That day with Uncle Gerald I found myself thinking, Dear God, I hope the day will come when

I'll be able to drive without being a threat to anyone else or myself. Please don't let me learn to drive until I can do so safely and without any symptoms of mental illness interfering.

Soon Kenny and I were on our way to Miami. He did not seem to be distressed about leaving his Des Moines parents. I felt assured I had the chance, once again, to be his mother.

Soon after we were back in Coconut Grove, Father took us out to dinner. He was thrilled to see his adorable grandson looking so well. He was also concerned about my welfare. "Liz, you really should get yourself a job. Your aunt and uncle can't continue to support you and Kenny for long." Father mentioned this to me as we left the restaurant.

"But, Dr. Goldberg doesn't want me to work until Kenny's been back with me longer," I told Father. "He said it wouldn't be good for Kenny to get back with me and then have me leave him every day for work."

Father went on, "Whenever your doctor feels you can leave Kenny to work you can get yourself a job. When you do, I'll be happy to write you a check for $25.00 each month."

That sure would be nice, I thought. It would be great to have some extra money.

A couple of months later I got a job with a small loan agency, and Father started sending me checks. I found the work very pressure-filled, and consequently, I only worked there three months. It was hectic getting up early each morning, getting Kenny ready, walking him over to Careton's Nursery School a couple of blocks away, and then catching the bus for downtown Miami. While working at the loan agency, I left Aunt Beth and Uncle Joseph's home, and Kenny and I went to live with Mother. All the pressure of childcare and work aggravated my relationships with my cousins and my aunt and uncle. I wanted to try and make a go of it again with Mom. I thought that maybe, for the first time in our lives, we could set up a home for the three of us. We would finally be living by ourselves as a family rather than living with relatives or a stepfather. I saw no reason why it wouldn't work, at least for now.

I knew it would be very hard for the three of us. Neither Mother nor I would have any income other than what we could earn working. We did not have the support of our ex-husbands, and I didn't know how much I could accomplish working since I was just getting over my illness. I also knew that one of us would have to provide care for Kenny. These thoughts weighed heavily on my already fragile mind.

Not long afterwards, Mom and I rented a small, two-bedroom duplex in the Grove. I started attending the "College and Career Group" at our church and dated several fellows I met at the group's Sunday evening meetings. I wondered whether my friends thought I was strange for having been hospitalized, but I utilized my reality-testing technique, which helped me not to worry. This paid off, because I found that by giving my friends the benefit of the doubt and not ascribing to them negative thoughts about me, I liked them better. I treated them without suspicion, and this helped them, in turn, to like me better.

****

"I wonder why you have such strong sexual feelings, Liz." Dr. Goldberg looked his usual pleasant self, but I could detect concern, as well, as he spoke to me that day in his office.

"I don't know," I responded. "Do I have stronger feelings than most people?"

"I think perhaps you do. But, from what you've told me about your sexual life, you've been more "good" and moral then most people. I don't believe I've ever known anyone who has lead as sexually moral life as you have."

As I thought about this conversation, I realized that I did have a struggle with my sexuality. I was a Christian who was trying to be sexually moral, but I was also a very passionate young woman. I did find myself very attracted to Dr. Goldberg, but he was always very proper in his behaviors.

"Dr. Goldberg I understand that my father has extremely strong sexual feelings, and that his mother was passionate. Maybe I inherited that aspect of my personality. Also, you'll remember I told you about the experiences I had as a child, the times Carl French-kissed me, and my episode with an uncle who who almost raped me when I was eleven."

"Yes, Liz, I do remember. It may be a result of the combination of your inherited traits and your life experiences. But, you don't need to be as good as you are sexually. Most young people can have sexual relationships with ten partners before they marry, and still have a good life with their mates when they do wed." My reaction to all of this was, I don't want to live that way. I don't want ten sexual partners. God doesn't want us to live like that.

Another man who suggested I have an active sexual life was my father. He told me about a friend of his who was a stewardess. She flew back and forth routinely from Florida to California. She had a lover in both states, having sexual relations with both of them. I wondered if the two men knew about the arrangement.

Father then said to me, "You should do something like that with your sex life, Liz."

That didn't appeal to me, however.

As for my religious beliefs during this period in my life, they lessened dramatically. I was still a Christian, but I had fallen into the trap we Christians fall into during hard times. I didn't understand why God, if He cared about His children, could let us suffer so much pain from physical, or especially, mental illnesses. I had learned that Christians were destined to live abundant lives. I certainly didn't feel my life had much that could be considered abundant other than abundant mental agony. I still went to church, but my faith was anything but fervent. Actually, I was a little mad at God.

Life continued for Mom, Kenny, and me there in Coconut Grove. We only lived in the duplex for three months. We'd moved there in late spring. The building wasn't air conditioned, and it was a hot box in the late spring and summer. We hunted around Coconut Grove until we found a nicer, two-bedroom duplex that was just a few dollars a month more. The second duplex had air conditioning. Delighted, we moved in and cooled down.

I needed to find a new job. I hadn't worked while lived in the first duplex, and by that time I needed to work for the three of us to get by financially. Mom had worked for a Jewish doctor for quite some time, Dr. Bernstein. She'd gone to work for him while I was in Iowa. He and his wife were good to her while I was in Jackson trying to recover from my mental illness. They were very understanding employers.

One day, not long after we moved into the new duplex, Mom said to me, "Liz, how would you like to work in our office part-time?"

"Your office?" I replied. "I didn't know you needed anyone."

"Carol Brady won't be returning to work this fall," she continued. "She takes the summers off, since we aren't busy enough to use her then. I mentioned to Dr. Bernstein that you need a part-time job and that you're a good typist, and he said he'd like to talk to you regarding working with us."

"Great, Mom! I'll go in with you tomorrow, if that's all right."

"Sure, that'll be fine."

I got the job, and really enjoyed working there. I worked for Dr. Bernstein for several months. Being at work was more like being at a country club. I was the receptionist in the mornings; I took in money and booked appointments. A lot of my time was spent socializing with the patients while they waited to see the doctor. Often they had to wait an hour or longer, so I helped them pass their time pleasantly. Most of Dr. Bernstein's patients were senior citizens who could wait a couple of hours to see him. Every Christmas, Dr. Bernstein's "girls" were showered with presents from the patients. Mom would usually bring home forty to fifty presents, and I received thirty or so myself that year. Dr. and Mrs. Bernstein were great people. He was one of the nicest men I'd ever worked for.

I had good days during the months I worked in Mom's office. But, I still wasn't completely satisfied. I got bored if things were slow at work. There were times when I thought that I should be doing something more with my life. I wanted to go to college and have a career that would be professional, but I couldn't figure out how I could accomplish something like that.

In the afternoons, I'd pick up Kenny from the nursery school. We'd walk all over the Grove, go to the dime store to buy a toy, and maybe to the Florida Pharmacy for a drink.

I had a bad habit during those days. I was still seeing Dr. Goldberg, of course, still searching for the "cure" to my mental malady. My bad habit was discussing my problems too much, even with strangers. Sometimes they seemed somewhat shocked, but usually they were broadminded. They often told me how "normal" I seemed to them.

I was still searching, and I was depressed much of the time. I'd get depressed whenever I thought about Carl and how he treated me during the thirteen years he and Mom were married. I talked a lot about Carl, and I often stated that I must be "no good," as he always had said. Relatives and friends would attempt to convince me that I really was a good person, but the imprint left by Carl remained.

One day, after Kenny and I returned from our afternoon stroll, I was particularly depressed. It seemed as though I could never keep up with all the housework, and I didn't even know where I was headed. Wouldn't I just be a mental patient forever? I didn't want to live anymore, because the struggle was just too much. I think I'll take something that will end it all. I know, I'll take several Trilafons.

"Kenny, go play in your room. Mommy is busy." I didn't want my son to see me taking the pills. He went to his room. I swallowed sixteen of the Trilafon pills. Then I lay on my bed, hoping to drift off into oblivion.

"Mommy, get up! Mommy, come on, get up!" Kenny was pulling at my clothes. Then I said to him, "I wish I was dead, Kenny. Please go away. I just want to lie here and die." I couldn't help feeling compassion for Kenny, but nevertheless, I said those terrible words to him.

"Liz! Liz! What's the matter with you? Why are you lying down now while Kenny is outside playing unsupervised?" Mom was nudging me as I lay there on my bed. She'd just arrived home from work.

"I took some Trilafon, Mom, sixteen of them."

"What? You what? You took sixteen Trilafon pills? Why on earth would you do that?"

"I don't know, Mom. I just don't know. I guess I wanted to die."

"Well, we'd better get you to the emergency room quick and have them pump out your stomach. Come on, get Kenny, and we'll go to the hospital. I don't know, Liz, what comes over you sometimes."

We went to Jackson, where I had my stomach pumped out. The doctor asked me some questions, and sent me home. Dr. Goldberg later told me that the amount of Trilafon I took couldn't kill anyone.

Dr. Goldberg and I decided I should go back into the hospital for a short stay. We both wanted me to get over my suicidal feelings.

I had also started having anxiety attacks. I would have an attack for no apparent reason, and they would last anywhere from one to three hours. During the attacks, I couldn't concentrate enough to work at anything, so I would lie down somewhere. After a while, I would usually dose off, and then after an hour or so I would be fine. I would feel great afterwards; all the anxiety would be gone. There never did seem to be any external event that triggered my attacks. They would just come, and then leave again after I'd lie down awhile.

Soon I was in Jackson again. Dr. Goldberg wasn't able to get me in the psychiatric wing immediately. He put me in the medical wing temporarily. The following day he came to see me.

"Hi, Liz. How are you feeling?"

"Fine, Dr. Goldberg. How are you?"

"Me? Oh, I'm all right. What have you been thinking about while lying around here?"

"You really want to know what I was thinking about?" I asked him.

"Yes, I do, Liz."

"Okay, then I'll tell you. I was thinking about you and me. Now, I know you're married, but I was day dreaming. I was thinking that I might be your patient for a long time, maybe even until you're quite old. Then I was thinking that maybe you will live longer than your wife. Then you'll be a widower one day and be available. I guess that really sounds crazy, but you wanted to know what I was thinking!"

"Liz, I'm your doctor, not your lover. But, yes it is true that I'm interested in what you think about. It's all part of what makes you, you. Anyway, I certainly hope we can help you get to feeling better while you're in the Institute. You do want to get well, don't you?"

"I don't know, Dr. Goldberg, sometimes I wonder about that."

"But, you must want to get well! That's the only way you can help yourself. You have to want to improve."

"I'll keep trying, Dr. Goldberg. I promise I will. You keep trying, too."

And Dr. Goldberg did keep trying. Even though technically he wasn't my doctor during this hospital-ization, since I was an inpatient, and he was doing his residency in the outpatient clinic, he saw me regard-less, simply because I wanted him to. I was assigned to a younger psychiatrist, Dr. Cohen, but I still went to see Dr. Goldberg for psychotherapy at the out-pa-tient clinic.

Soon afterwards, I was admitted to the Institute. While there, I was given a battery of psychological tests. I didn't learn the results, but while I took the test I felt very sexy, and I projected those feeling into the test, giving importance to male dominance.

I was in Jackson only a week or two. Dr. Goldberg gave me an excellent recommendation to Dr. Bernstein over the phone while I sat in Dr. Goldberg's office. I was pleased he thought so highly of me and cared enough to say nice things about me to my boss. Soon I was home again with Mom and Kenny, back working in the country-club-like medical office.

Chapter Fifteen

OUT OF THE PIT

Hollywood, Florida, 1965

When I came home from my second stay in the Institute, I continued being tormented by suicidal thoughts. I attempted suicide again, for the third time. This time I was more serious. I knew Trilafon would not kill me, so I decided to take rat poison. I walked down to the store, and searched the shelves for the poison that would end my suffering. I bought the poison, and headed back to our duplex, where I swallowed about two tablespoons, the amount I thought was enough to kill me.

Waiting to die, I lay down on my bed. Again I said those awful words to Kenny, "I wish I was dead, Kenny. Please go away. I just want to lie here and die." Poor Kenny! What traumatic experiences my second and third suicide attempts must have been for his young, impressionable mind.

Once again Mom found me, on her return home from work, lying down, and not supervising my son. "What are you doing, Liz? Did you take something to kill yourself again?" Mom asked in shock and fear.

"Yes, Mom, I'm afraid I took rat poison; it's on the kitchen counter."

Mom called Dr. Bernstein to ask about an antidote for the poison, and to find out whether we should go to the hospital. He told her what I should take and that hospitalization wasn't necessary. I took the antidote, and failed in my third attempt at suicide. When I took the Trilafon, I didn't really expect to die. With the rat poison, I fully expected and hoped to pass into nothingness.

By this time, all three of us, Mom, Dr. Goldberg, and I felt I should be hospitalized again for a sufficient length of time to effect a cure. We all agreed that these suicide attempts had to stop; we needed a permanent solution.

Dr. Goldberg suggested to Mom that she take a more serious step than she'd taken in the past. He suggested she have the court certify me incompetent and place me in a hospital for a six-month period. He felt I should be hospitalized for at least that long in order for me to get over my depression. If I needed to be in the hospital at the end of the six months, I would then be committed by the courts for an indefinite stay.

Although Uncle Joseph was concerned about Mom's certifying me incompetent through the courts, Dr. Goldberg told Mom that there might be no other choice if I were to be helped, and hopefully cured. She went ahead and instituted proceedings.

Mom also faced the problem of Kenny's care during the six-month period of my pending hospitalization. We considered the possibility of making him a ward of the court and having him cared for in a home for dependent children while I would be gone. A social worker at Jackson advised against this, however, for Kenny's sake. He suggested Mom should find some way to care for Kenny, without resorting to putting him in a home.

Jane, my friend from my first stay in the Institute, was looking for a place to stay at that time, as she'd just been released from South Florida State Hospital. Mom came up with a plan to rent my room to Jane, with kitchen privileges, to help pay the bills and keep

Kenny at home. Jane liked the idea, and moved into the Grove duplex with Mom and Kenny.

Since I would have to await the court hearing, Dr. Goldberg decided to have me admitted somewhere else, temporarily. I checked into the Retreat one afternoon in the spring of 1965. I spoke to the staff doctor, who asked me if I was taking any medications. I told him I was taking three 4-mg Trilafon pills each day. He wrote down the information, and said I could continue taking Trilafon. I asked him if he was a psychiatrist, and he told me that he was not a psychiatrist, but that he was a medical doctor.

****

"This will be your room for tonight, Liz." The attendant opened the door to a small room with a bed and not much else except for a strange looking apparatus lying on the bed.

"What's that thing?"

"Oh, that's a 'straight jacket,'" she replied. "Every new patient has to wear one their first night here." I didn't particularly mind the thought of having to wear the jacket, but I intended to be on my best behavior so that I wouldn't have to wear it more than one night. I didn't sleep well with my arms stretched out, my legs apart and straight. I usually slept well, for which I felt grateful. Had I been a restless sleeper, I would have had an awful night!

The next morning they unstrapped the jacket and led me to another room, where other patients sat. I was told this is the first room patients stay in until it is determined which section of the building they are assigned.

I looked around and surveyed my companions. What a bunch of emaciated human beings, I thought. They looked like the elderly patients at Uncle Gerald's nursing home. They're not that old though, I thought, and they're so thin. I decided they must be in bad shape. I began talking to some of the more alert-looking patients. I learned that the patients who looked so bad had been in that section of the Retreat for a long time. They looked like they were very mentally ill, and some of them never talked. The next day the staff physician, Dr. Weatherly, came back to see me.

"How have you been feeling, Liz?"

"Oh, fine," I replied. "I was wondering if maybe I could try getting by without taking my Trilafon. I'm feeling quite well, and I was doing pretty well before I came in here, working a job and all. Maybe I don't need the medicine anymore."

"Well, it's fine with me if you want to try going without it. I agree that you seem quite healthy."

"Thanks, Dr. Weatherly."

The next day I was moved to the "best" section of the building, where I was given a private room with my own marble-tiled bathroom. I had the only room with a mirror over the dresser. I felt special. I must have made a good impression on the "powers that be," I thought. After all, I was still functioning pretty well. I had been without my medicine for one day.

There wasn't much to do in the Retreat, very little stimulation and no recreation. I looked forward to eating breakfast each morning. They were delicious, with pancakes, bacon and eggs, and so forth. There was a television set in a small dayroom, where I watched TV and played cards with other patients. We were allowed on the sun porch once a day, and I enjoyed spending time there. Other than that, I sat around looking at the walls or talking to other patients.

Mom came to visit me every weekend. A friend of mine named Pete Goldman visited me several times, also. We'd dated before I entered the Retreat. He was divorced and had two teenage daughters. He was interested in my illness because he'd experienced depression and mild suicidal feelings himself, although he'd never been hospitalized. He was somewhat fascinated with my case, and we had become close.

Jane visited one Sunday with Mom. I was impressed with how well she seemed to be doing. She was taking quite a bit of medicine that had been given to her from the State Hospital. She had a job she enjoyed, and so far, things were going all right between her and Mom.

As the days and weeks went by, I began noticing problems, symptomatic in nature. I found that I was beginning to have thoughts very similar to those I'd had before and during my hospitalization in Iowa. People were turning into Communists, and I again thought that the Lord's return was at hand. It interested me that I was having almost identical delusions as my original ones.

I had periods in my days when I would realize that my thoughts were inaccurate and symptomatic of mental Illness. When this would happen, I would decide to ask Dr. Weatherly to put me back on my medicine. The only problem with this was that his visits to our section coincided with my "sickest" periods. He always seemed to be there while I was feeling sure my delusions were true. It was during his absences that I would realize I needed to talk to him, but he didn't visit at those times. I would have had to initiate speaking to him about the problem, during his visits, but I never did.

I was gradually descending again into the depths of insanity. Although there were periods when I was aware something was wrong, my awareness gradually slipped away, and I found myself back in the throes of madness. One thing was certain, if I was insane, at least I was in a sanctuary for the insane.

I needed more to do to occupy my time, so I got a novel and started reading. It was interesting, and I became engrossed in the romantic aspects of the story. Before long, however, I put the book down and began to daydream. I found myself thinking that I really enjoy sex. But, there isn't much chance of anything like that in here. My mind became disjointed again, as it had been in Iowa. I continued daydreaming in the same crazy manner. I wondered what it would be like to be a prostitute. In my mind, I thought it might not be so bad.

I found myself repeating these thoughts about prostitution, and adding to them some of the flavor of my delusions. The Communists are going to force me into prostitution because I am rather pretty, I decided. They will give this job to me in their new order after they take over the United States. Maybe I should learn to accept the inevitable. I entertained these unusual thoughts during a fair amount of my time in the Retreat.

One day, a week or so after I'd started having these sexually flavored delusions, I decided to write to Dr. Goldberg. The plot and conspiracy aspects of my paranoid delusions were prompting me to ask him for help, for a means of escape from my persecutors. I wrote and told him that Communists were taking over the Retreat, that they wanted people to become homosexuals, but that I would be spared because they wanted to make me a prostitute. I didn't hear back from Dr. Goldberg, and I couldn't figure out why. I thought that maybe the letter had gotten lost, because I believed Dr. Goldberg would want to help me out of this terrible situation. I remained hopeful that the letter would still get to him.

Aunt Beth came all the way from Coconut Grove to the Retreat to visit me one afternoon. My lack of friendliness and warmth disappointed her. I was so involved in my own little world of imaginary thoughts that I hardly realized she'd come to see me.

A few days later, the court sent two people, at different times, to see me and assess my competency before I went before the judge. One man asked sharply about my three suicide attempts, "Why would you try to kill yourself three times?"

I didn't answer him. I wondered, why does he have to talk to me so accusingly? Does he think I was trying to kill myself because I enjoyed the thought of killing? Doesn't he realize that I'm crying out for help, for a cure from my insanity? He must believe I'm worthless. Maybe that's true. Maybe I'm just no good, period.

I did make friends with two or three of the other patients in the Retreat. I spent lots of time with a teenage girl named Janice. We played cards a lot, and talked. She always fussed at me for being too "perfect." She was there for substance abuse and suicide attempts. Then there was the middle-aged woman who had delirium tremens one night while lying in her bed. She was an alcoholic, and there were several other alcoholics receiving treatment in the Retreat. I also met an elderly woman who thought people were trying to get in her window. She was scared to death. Finally, her doctor gave her several shock treatments, and she recovered enough to leave for home. Someone told me that that particular doctor gave shock treatments to most of his patients. I was thankful he wasn't my doctor. I'd never had shock treatments, and I didn't want to start having them.

I was in the Retreat for approximately one month before going before the judge with Mom. He was to be the one to decide where I would go, Jackson Institute where Dr. Goldberg hoped I would be placed, or South Florida State Hospital in Hollywood, Florida.

I didn't realize that a police officer would escort me to the hearing, so I was rather surprised when he arrived. "Hello, are you Elizabeth Martino?" The nice-looking man speaking to me looked rather friendly and personable. I lost any fear of him I otherwise might have had.

"Yes, that's my name. Who are you?"

"I'm Jason Lesley. I'll be going with you today to the courthouse."

"Am I going before the judge today, already?"

"Yes, Elizabeth. I'll give you a minute or two to get ready, then we better leave. The car is waiting outside. Just meet me here by the door when you're ready."

"Okay, Jason. Thanks."

So, today's the big day before the judge, I thought. I wonder if I should confide in him and tell him about what's been going on in this place. Oh, well, Dr. Goldberg hasn't even answered my letter yet. Maybe it's all in my head again. I wish I knew for sure. I better just ask for help, and hope the judge does help me with all my problems.

I went to the door to meet Jason. He was waiting for me, smiling. "Well, that didn't take long," he said. "We'll have plenty of time to get to the courthouse."

As we drove along through the northern part of Miami and south into Miami proper, Jason and I talked and got acquainted with each other. He seemed to like me, and he helped me lose any fear I had of the ordeal ahead. As we rode through the downtown streets, I looked out the car window and thought that, yes, the end of the world is definitely drawing near. Jason and I continued to converse at the courthouse. After waiting for about a half hour, I was taken into a room with the judge, Mom, and a court reporter.

The judge was a middle-aged man. He looked kindly. He turned to me and said, "What is your name, Miss?"

"Elizabeth, Elizabeth Martino, Sir," I replied.

"I understand you've had some trouble for a year or two," he continued, "some emotional or mental problems?"

"Yes, I have. I've been hospitalized four times since 1962. But I'm still sick." It was a relief to come before the judge and express my needs to him.

"What hospitals were you in?"

"I was in Blythe Memorial Hospital in Iowa two times. Then I was in the Institute at Jackson Memorial Hospital twice, once in 1963, and then again, just a few months ago."

"I understand also," the judge continued, "that you're troubled with a low opinion of yourself, that somehow you feel you're 'no good.' Is that correct?"

"Yes, it is sir."

Mom spoke up then, commenting on my self-concept. "Elizabeth learned from her step-father, during the thirteen years he and I were married, that she was 'no good.' He was always telling her that, and she now believes it. We're having trouble convincing her that it's not true. I would very much like to see her have, as her doctor states, a healthier self-concept."

"Yes," the judge replied, "if she actually has such low self-esteem, she should definitely receive some help." Then, looking at me, he said, "Elizabeth, I am certifying you to a six-month stay at South Florida State Hospital in Hollywood."

With that over, Jason escorted me back to the Retreat. When he left me that afternoon, he said he hoped I'd get the care and help I wanted, that he'd enjoyed meeting and talking with me. I left Jason, thankful we'd met. He'd been refreshingly normal.

When I got to my room, I lay down. I'd been doing a lot of that. It was part of my usual behavior whenever my illness was active. I soon found myself thinking about my pending hospitalization. I'm finally going to be in a state hospital, I thought. It's about time. Even though my doctor wanted to care for me again in Jackson and fought for that, I'm glad I'm going to Hollywood. I have a feeling help is there for me. I think all this end-of-the-world business is probably just craziness again. I wish something would be invented, some medicine or something, which would cure my insanity. "Please, God in Heaven, please let a medicine or medicines be invented that will solve this problem. I know Dr. Goldberg says I shouldn't look to pills for my cure, but, Dear God, I don't know where else to look. Something has to help me. Please God, please answer my prayer."

The next day, another policeman escorted me to Hollywood, Florida, to the State Hospital. Mom went up in her car, so she could be with me while I was being admitted.

I was impressed with the appearance of the hospital grounds. I had been at South Florida State Hospital one time before, to visit Jane when she was a patient there, so the hospital was not new to me. After I was admitted, I was taken to the admitting ward. It was a typical "first ward" of a mental hospital. Whereas most of the buildings at this hospital were cottages, this ward was in a larger building, which had locked doors.

"Hello, Elizabeth. I'm Dr. Chambers. How are you today?"

"Oh, I'm all right, I guess." I replied to the nice-looking, middle-aged man standing in front of me.

"Would you please come with me to my office for a few minutes?" he continued. "I need to get some information." There Dr. Chambers asked me several questions.

Oh well, I thought, at least this isn't as bad as what I went through this morning when I had to strip before those two women. They asked me all sorts of medical questions and then told me they had to check to see if I had any bruises. I found this process embarrassing. At least Dr. Chambers apparently doesn't expect me to strip.

"Are you taking any medications, Elizabeth?" I brought myself mentally back to my conversation with the doctor and answered his question.

"No, and I don't want to take any, either. The medicine is just poison the Communists want me to take. I know it is!"

"Elizabeth, the medicine is not poison. I want you to take Stelazine. It will be given to you in liquid form at first. I'm also going to prescribe some iron for you because you're anemic. We're through for now. Come on, I'll take you back out to the dayroom, where some of the other patients are watching television."

Yuck, I thought, he's going to make me take that poisonous medicine. I don't suppose I can refuse it, either; that would just get me in deeper trouble. Maybe it's really not poison. I guess I'll soon find out, since he's making me take it.

I sat down in one of the chairs in the dayroom. Dr. Chambers said, "Goodbye," and left. I watched him leave, feeling hatred for him as my newest Communist persecutor.

As the first few days went by, I was bothered by a simple word in the English language, the word "she." I sat in the dayroom, not particularly talking to anyone. I heard the conversations of the other patients. It seemed as though every time a woman said "she's ..." I thought the "she" was me. Evidentially everyone is talking about me, I decided. I must make fascinating gossip. My head was reeling from hearing so many "she's ..." The trouble was I heard just that word and not much else.

About the third day I was in the admitting ward, a young man asked me if I wanted to go to a dance that

Recreation Therapy was giving. I told him I'd love to and walked off with him to a nearby room.

I felt sexy that day. All my clothes had been taken for marking, so I didn't have a bra right then to wear. I was wearing a cotton dress the staff had given me, with just panties under it. I wasn't in the habit of going without a bra, normally, but I felt very free and easy that afternoon dancing with the fellows, especially when I danced with the handsome young therapist. The next day I received my clothes back.

After I'd been in the state hospital for a couple of weeks, I went before a staffing committee. When the chief psychiatrist asked me what had caused my condition, I'm sure that my answer sounded strange.

"My mother," I told her. "When I was a very small child we slept together in the same bed. She molested me. That's what made me sick, and that's why I ended up in here."

Soon, I was moved to a cottage. It was great to live more in the open, although the doors to this cottage were kept locked most of the time. We were allowed to leave the cottage for work, therapies, and meals. If I improved and behaved well, I would one day be able to move up to an unlocked cottage, and then I could come and go on my own.

Before long, my days were filled with activities. There was charm school, recreation therapy, occupational therapy, and parties with the men's cottages. Soon I would be interviewed for a job.

Not everything was positive in my head, however. I believed my food was poisonous and didn't eat my meals. We walked up to the cafeteria en masse, military style. Once we got there, I often refused to eat. One good thing about my not eating was that I became very slender and looked great. As soon as I was allowed to be around the male patients, I became quite popular. One night a beau stole a kiss and later on another young man proposed.

The first job I was assigned to was helping Recreation Therapy. It involved participating with other patients in sports, parties, dances, and so on. I worked with the therapists. We weren't paid for our work, but jobs helped defray expenses. I was indigent, and didn't pay for my stay.

I found myself getting fatigued walking around on my job, playing sports. Most of the time when I arrived home to the cottage from work, I would lie down on the couch with unusual thoughts running through my head. Boy, I sure am tired. And, there's still so much going on leading up to the end of the world, or it seems that way, anyhow, if I'm not crazy again and imagining all of this.

I'm sure glad I can't go home weekends for the first few months, I thought. I'm so afraid I'd hurt Kenny if I went home now. I'm afraid I'd get up in the middle of the night, go out to the kitchen, get a butcher knife, and hurt him. I wouldn't want to do that. I'm just afraid my impulses would get the best of me. It would be so terrible if I did hurt Kenny. I would never be able to live with myself if I did something like that, even if I were not put to death because I'm insane. That's why I am so glad that this hospital won't let me go home for a while. Maybe by the time I'm allowed to go home, I'll be over these feelings. I hope so.

I saw Dr. Chambers for about fifteen to twenty minutes, once a week. I asked him if it would be possible for me to have psychotherapy sessions with him. He told me, no, that he was sorry, he had to see and take care of one hundred patients, which didn't allow him enough time for any psychotherapy with us.

I told him how much I'd gotten out of my therapy sessions with Dr. Goldberg. Dr. Chambers then told me that he had supervised Dr. Goldberg while he was doing his residency at this hospital, and he happened to know that I was "special" to Dr. Goldberg. That statement made my day.

Later that same day, one of the aides told me there was a gentleman to see me. She brought him over to me in the dayroom.

"Hello, Mrs. Martino?"

"Yes, I'm Liz Martino."

I'm Rev. Bell, a minister at one of the local churches. I understand you're a member of a Congregational Church in Miami."

"Yes," I replied. "Actually, the church I belong to is in Coconut Grove."

"I was out in this neighborhood," Rev. Bell continued, "and just thought I'd stop by the hospital to visit a few people. How long have you been here?"

"About two months," I answered. "I've been a psychiatric patient for a few years now. I'm hoping that I'll get the help I need here."

"Do you go to church here, Liz?"

"Yes," I replied, "I usually attend the Sunday morning services here. I also attended Bible College for one year in 1958–1959. But, I find that if I get too involved with religion, it's not always so good for me. In fact, when I have delusions with my illness, they're usually religious in nature. I don't know why it is that my mind tends to distort something which is so great, faith in God and in Jesus."

"There must be more to it than you've been able to discern so far, Liz. I agree with you that it does seem hard to understand. I'm sure things will work out for you."

Rev. Bell and I talked a while longer before he left. It felt strange talking to him as a state mental patient, especially since so much of my delusional thinking revolved around concepts I'd learned from the Bible and in Bible college. But, I thought it was nice that he had taken time out of his busy schedule to visit me.

I was reaching the point mentally when sometimes I was involved with my delusions, but at other times, I was not preoccupied with them. I was beginning to realize that I was again mentally ill, and that the terrible things I had been thinking were about to happen were just figments of my imagination.

Depression was beginning to replace the imaginary thoughts. I was also beginning to have more of my unexplainable anxiety attacks.

What was bothering me the most was that I was having impulsive feelings about hurting other people. I had feelings of wanting to lash out at someone, anyone, who happened to be nearby. Right away, however, I would resist these temptations because I believed that if I hurt anyone, I should have to suffer severe consequences in return; it wouldn't matter that I committed these actions while insane. These thoughts deterred my actions of violence. I asked Dr. Chambers to put me on Trilafon rather than Stelazine. I told him that I had found in the past that Trilafon helped me the most. He agreed to put me on Trilafon, and the change did seem to help some.

Mom and Kenny visited me on weekends. I wasn't very receptive to them, because my anxiety attacks always seemed to interfere with their visits. Mom was patient with me, for which I was thankful, and she continued coming and bringing Kenny each weekend.

Pete came to visit me a few times while I was in the State Hospital. On one visit, he told me he thought he was in love with me. But, I wasn't much fun for him to be with nor did I give him any encouragement. He came a couple of times and after that didn't return. The hospital was a long drive from Miami, especially when I was negative.

Dr. Chambers was becoming more of a confidante for me. He really was a nice doctor, and a good man. He wanted me to have more trust in people, and he also wanted me to realize that many people imagine things from time to time, in varying degrees. I couldn't help thinking that my particular problem with imaginary thoughts was far more serious than any difficulties the average person might have.

My anxiety attacks didn't let up. One day, I didn't feel like going to work, so I didn't go. I'd been working in the clothing room in the afternoons for two months. My attacks interfered with my work there. I thought, that afternoon, that if I didn't go to work, I wouldn't have to face the problem of having any anxiety attacks on the job.

Then, that night, I did something even more drastic. I refused to go to dinner when it was time for us to go. The attendant wasn't pleased with my behavior. She informed me that I would probably be sent back to a locked cottage. I'd been living in an open cottage for two months.

Dr. Chambers had me returned to a locked cottage. My first night there was quite an ordeal. I had an awful anxiety attack that lasted the entire night. I felt the same impulsive feelings of wanting to lash out at others, but I never did.

Dr. Chambers told me the next day that he felt I had a chemical imbalance and that, therefore, he was going to increase my medication. He said he felt that my anxiety attacks were also due to this imbalance. He put me on both Stelazine and Trilafon, plus Cogentin for the side effects. Before I'd taken only Trilafon with Cogentin. I noticed within a few days that I was feeling considerably better, and my anxiety attacks lessened.

It seemed to me that my suffering brain had improved. One afternoon, I decided to read some of the printed sermons by the minister from Aunt Beth's church that she had given me. I was experiencing a return of the desire to look to God for help. I read two sermons and felt encouraged.

One day, not long after this, I was eating lunch in the cafeteria with a good friend of mine named Ruth.

Ruth's particular problem had been an extremely serious depression. She hadn't imagined things as I had, but she'd attempted suicide several times.

As we sat together that day, Ruth told me about a good development in her care. "Liz, I've finally found a cure for my depression. I never thought I would, but I have!"

A cure for depression, I thought. I doubt if my suicidal depression could ever be cured. I wonder what Ruth's cure is.

"Ruth, what is your new cure?"

"Aventyl," she replied. "It's a new medication that has just come out. My depression has cleared up since I've been taking it."

"That's great!" I told her. "Maybe I should ask Dr. Chambers to let me try your new medicine. How do you spell the name?"

"A-v-e-n-t-y-l," she answered.

"Okay, thanks a lot!"

The following day Dr. Chambers saw me and asked how I was feeling. I told him I was feeling quite a bit better, but I still had some depression. I mentioned what Ruth had said about the Aventyl. Dr.

Chambers decided to try me on Aventyl along with Stelazine, Trilafon, and Cogentin.

That week, the week that Dr. Chambers placed me on that combination of medicine, was the healthiest week of my entire life! I had no more delusions and absolutely no depression or suicidal thoughts, or thoughts of hurting others. I was no longer a mentally ill woman. I was perfectly normal in my personality and behavior.

I went from not wanting to go to one, three-hour job each day, to working two jobs daily. Instead of avoiding physical activity and work, I walked all around the grounds two to three times daily, and asked for extra work assignments in my cottage. I moved back to an open cottage.

One of the best results was that I lost my depression for good. Life then was positive; it was, for a change, good to be alive. Within two weeks of the addition of Aventyl to the Stelazine and Trilafon, I felt better than I'd ever felt. I was a whole and new person.

Some changes were happening to Mom during this time, as well. She'd been seeing a psychiatric nurse at the public health department. This nurse had bolstered Mom's self-confidence. She told Mom that she was right in her ideas of what I needed, that she had been with me during my growing years and all the years with Carl. The nurse felt that Mom understood my situation better than anyone else did.

This helped Mom greatly. She had been feeling that she was the one to blame for my condition, as some of our relatives had told her. With this nurse's bolstering, Mom took new courage, and stepped out into new life with me, confident that both she and I could cope with our lives and raise Kenny.

Six months after I was certified to South Florida State Hospital as incompetent, I was released with my competency restored. Before I left, Mom met with Dr. Chambers to discuss my future. He told her that it was evident to him that my serious and suicidal depression was what he called "endogenous," or organic. He believed that was the reason the antidepressant Aventyl had cured my depression. He also said that I would need to take this combination of psychiatric medicine for the rest of my life, unless my condition were to improve when I would go through menopause.

Finally, I was cured, at least with the help of the medications. God had answered the prayers I'd prayed that day in the Retreat, six months before. Everything looked wonderful to me. I was a healed mental patient. Bright days lay ahead.

Chapter Sixteen

FORTY-FIVE YEARS WITH MY SOUND MIND

Orlando, 2011

"Mathieu, Kenny's Memorial Service was really beautiful, wasn't it?"

"Yes, Liz it was. The ministers spoke very highly of him, and many people came even though he was homebound for his last four years. It was nice to see many of his ambulance drivers show up.

"Kenny had such a wonderful attitude, as sick as he was. I never heard him complain about the misery he experienced. Even toward the end of his life, he never expressed anger about his situation, and he never blamed God."

"That's very true, Mat. He always testified to his faith in God and God's will for him. He loved the visits from the ministers when they would come over to give him communion and sing spiritual songs to him."

"That was good of them. It's hard to believe he passed away before his fiftieth birthday. He was still a young man. How many years was Kenny on dialysis altogether, Liz?"

"Thirty-one years. He started getting sick thirty-six years ago, when he was thirteen. We had just moved from Miami to Orlando, when he started having pains in his legs. His condition was serious, and he had several surgeries, but the cause of his symptoms was not determined for four years. It wasn't until things got very severe that new doctors discovered that his bone disease was due to kidney failure."

"Do you know what caused Kenny's kidney failure?"

"We weren't sure. He was a healthy baby, and healthy during all his elementary school years. I don't know of anyone in my family with kidney problems, and my ex-husband, Mario, told me he knew of no one in his family with kidney problems. Ken did have an accident on a dirt bike when he was twelve, and we wondered if he may have injured a kidney then."

"You told me once, Liz, that many years ago you suffered from mental illness. I don't see any signs of illness with you now or since I have gotten to know you while working with Kenny these past eight months. I know it must have been hard on you caring for Kenny all these years, especially the past four years when he suffered the most. It seems to me this would've only been possible if you possessed a sound mind. Tell me more about your experiences with mental illness. Did it affect Kenny?"

"It began fifty years ago, when I came down with schizophrenia. In fact, my original diagnosis was paranoid schizophrenia. But, miraculously, four years later I was placed on a combination of psychiatric medications that healed me within just a few days. I had prayed to God that a medicine would be invented that would cure my mental illness. An antidepressant came out that year which, when combined with the anti-schizophrenia medicine I was already taking, resulted in my cure. My mental condition was not only schizophrenia. I was also depressed and suicidal, so I needed healing from that, as well.

"I've taken the medicine ever since, and I've been able to live a normal and successful life. With the help of the medicine, over the past forty-seven years, I earned a bachelor's degree in Special Education, another bachelor's degree in Psychology, and seven years ago, I earned a Masters of Arts degree in Mental Health Counseling.

"I worked for the State of Florida for eighteen years as a special education teacher, and then as a human services counselor. After getting my MA degree in counseling, I worked with persons suffering from mental illnesses until 2007. Then I had to quit the few hours a week I was working, because Ken had become so ill that I needed to be with him all the time.

"Ken didn't remember my mental illness experiences. He was only four years old when I was healed. I'm sure somewhere in the gray matter of his brain something was recorded during his first four years, but he couldn't recall my insanity when I asked him. Even when I was ill, I was a good mother. Through taking my medicine, I was able to overcome my illness and his life with me became normal and healthy.

"Mom and I raised Kenny together. We were both divorced, and neither of us remarried. Mom died in 2002. She developed dementia during her late eighties, and I cared for her as well as caring for Ken. She passed away at age ninety-three.

"Kenny loved my mother so much. She was a tremendous help for him and me. I don't know what Kenny and I would have done without her.

"So, you see, Mat, even though I once was very mentally Ill, God rescued me in many ways, especially making sure I received the right medication.

"I wish every person with a psychotic condition, whether it be delusions or hallucinations, could get the medicine they need, and continue taking it. I myself did not hallucinate, but I did have delusions.

"There was a brief period in 1976, when I tried to go off my medicine. I prayed that God would heal me without my having to take any medication. I always took my pills three times a day, but I went a day and a half without taking any medicine. Then I realized I needed to go back on my medication, because I began having delusions again. This was the first time in eleven years that I had experienced delusions. Evidently, God's plan was for me to keep taking my medicine.

"I did have some residual anger toward God when I was ill, and even several years after my healing. I was upset because He let me experience madness for four years, and I was upset for having to suffer from my condition. For a long time, I didn't even give Him the praise for answering my prayers in providing me healing medicine. I'd forgotten I had prayed for that. Later I remembered.

"Prior to my illness, I was very active as a Christian, but it took several years before my strong faith returned. I've discovered that the longer I have known God and experienced His faithfulness, the more He means to me, and I am very happy now with my close relationship with God.

"Anyhow, Mat, that's my story."

Mat looked so kind and caring as we talked. He was only twenty-three, yet he was so thoughtful and mature. As we talked more about Kenny and reflected on his life, Mat reassured me that my son was now free from the physical suffering of his frail body.

Mat had come to work for Kenny and me because I developed problems with my ankle and foot. It became too difficult for me to take care of Kenny, between his developed abscesses, his tracheotomy, his oxygen, and other problems that developed from being bound to a bed for several years. Since Mat was going to school to become a nurse, it was comforting to have him there.

"Mat, you have been absolutely wonderful in providing the care we needed. I can never thank you enough."

With Ken's passing, he left behind a large collection of valuable toys, comics, and other collectibles. I knew he had had a desire to open a store, but with all of his illnesses, it would have never been possible. I wonder if Mat would be interested in helping me sell Kenny's collectibles, I thought.

"Mat, Kenny left me his collection. Would you be interested in helping me sell it? I know he treasured these items and loved collecting them, but they've literally taken over this house. I know you have some experience with computers; would you like to continue working for me?"

"I would love to, Liz. I know Kenny collected many valuable things. How did he afford that? What was his main source of income?"

"Well, it was highly unusual. I would just say it was a wonderful blessing from God."

"I guess he was very blessed in that aspect, but I'm sure he would have traded all that for good health."

I looked at Mat and nodded in agreement.

I wasn't too depressed at Kenny's passing. He died once before, briefly in 1995, and had a wonderful experience with God. Toward the end of his life he had gotten so terribly ill and suffered so greatly, it was a blessing that God took him home. I know I will see him again; he will be without abscesses, he will be walking, and he will be smiling his wonderful smile.

EPILOGUE
2014

Orlando

I am Rosemary Ross. I wrote this book about my life. I belonged to a writers club called the Midnight Oil Burners' Society, for several years. The members were a great help. Also, my friend, Mathieu, who is like a grandson to me, assisted with the final version. Elizabeth, or "Liz," is the name I use for myself in this book. Now, forty-nine years later, I look back over all the years during which I've been mentally healthy. I have been a woman with a sound mind, no longer mentally ill.

Since losing my son, I have recently moved into a retirement center. I am very happy here and have hundreds of friends. I keep myself very active both mentally and physically.

I hope by telling my story that I've shed some light on how my mental illness developed. The love and care I received from my true, natural family has helped me relearn to love myself. My return to my biblical Christian faith has been my most recent healing force. I have grown fond of Gospel music and Christian ministries, both of which have become a big part of my life now and continue to help me heal. I still believe, however, that the medicines I've been given are the main healing factors in my cure. Please, mental health consumers, if your medicine cures your delusions or hallucinations, keep taking it. May every psychiatric patient have a bright future.

CPSIA information can be obtained
at www.ICGtesting.com
Printed in the USA
LVOW04s1242011016
506943LV00001B/1/P